Science

Daily Practice Workbook

20 weeks of fun activities

2nd

ARGOPREP

 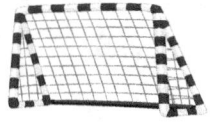    

Physical Science • **Life Science** • **Earth & Space Science** • **Engineering**

ArgoPrep is one of the leading providers of supplemental educational products and services. We offer affordable and effective test prep solutions to educators, parents and students. Learning should be fun and easy! To access more resources visit us at www.argoprep.com.

Our goal is to make your life easier, so let us know how we can help you by e-mailing us at: info@argoprep.com.

- ArgoPrep is a recipient of the prestigious **Mom's Choice Award**.

- ArgoPrep also received the 2019 **Seal of Approval** from Homeschool.com for our award-winning workbooks.

- ArgoPrep was awarded the 2019 **National Parenting Products Award**, **Gold Medal Parent's Choice Award** and the **Tillywig Brain Child Award**.

SCIENCE SERIES

Science Daily Practice Workbook by ArgoPrep is an award-winning series created by certified science teachers to help build mastery of foundational science skills. Our workbooks explore science topics in depth with ArgoPrep's 5 E'S to build science mastery.

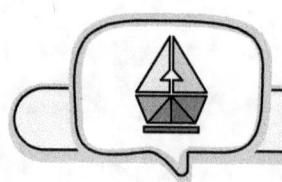
Introduction

Welcome to our 2nd grade science workbook!

This workbook is for 2nd grade students studying the Next Generation Science Standards. Included are 20 weeks of comprehensive instruction, working through the four branches of science: Physical Science, Life Science, Earth and Space Science and Engineering.

This workbook dedicates several weeks of instruction to each of the four branches of science, focusing on different standards within each week of instruction.

Within the branch of Physical Science, students will study matter, chemical reactions, light and sound. In Life Science, they will learn more about the water cycle, different animals, and the survival and adaptation of organisms in their environments. Students will dive into the four seasons, the solar system and erosion in Earth and Space Science. Finally, in the Engineering section, they will have the opportunity to become an engineer and design a robot aimed at solving a problem in their life.

At the conclusion of the 20 weeks of instruction, students should have a solid grasp on the concepts required of the Next Generation Science Standards for 2nd grade.

Table of Contents

How to Use the Book . . . . Page 4

Weekly Planner . . . . Page 6

List of Topics . . . . Page 7

Daily Activity Pages . . . . .Page 12

Answer Key . . . . .Page 181

How to Use the Book

All 20 weeks of daily activity pages in this book follow the same weekly structure. The book is divided into four sections: Physical Science, Life Science, Earth & Space Science and Engineering. The activities in each of the sections align to the Next Generation Science Standards which will help prepare students for state standardized assessments. While the sections can be completed in any order, it is important to complete each week within the section in chronological order, as the skills often build upon one another.

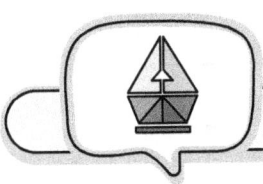 **argoprep.com**

Each week focuses on one specific topic within the section. More information about the weekly structure can be found in the Weekly Planner section.

How to access video explantions?

Go to **argoprep.com/science2**
OR scan the QR Code:

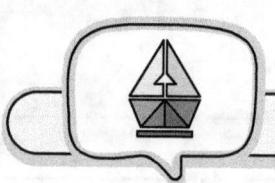

Weekly Planner

Day	Activity	Description
1	Engaging with the Topic	Read a short text on the topic and answer multiple choice questions.
2	Exploring the Topic	Interact with the topic on a deeper level by collecting, analyzing and interpreting data.
3	Explaining the Topic	Make sense of the topic by explaining and beginning to draw conclusions about the data.
4	Experimenting with the Topic	Investigate the topic through hands-on, easy to implement experiments.
5	Elaborating on the Topic	Reflect on the topic and use all information learned to draw conclusions and evaluate results.

List of Topics

Unit	Week	Topic
Physical Science	1	Classifying Matter Based on Hardness, Weight, Texture and Flexibility
Physical Science	2	Classifying Matter Based on Strength, Force and Hardness
Physical Science	3	Chemical Reactions and States of Matter
Physical Science	4	The Characteristics of Light
Physical Science	5	Sound
Life Science	6	Vertebrates and Invertebrates
Life Science	7	The Water Cycle
Life Science	8	Plants & Pollinators
Life Science	9	Plants Structures & Functions
Life Science	10	Habitats
Life Science	11	Adaptation & Survival
Life Science	12	The Sun and Light on Earth
Earth & Space Science	13	Erosion
Earth & Space Science	14	Natural Disasters
Earth & Space Science	15	Seasons
Earth & Space Science	16	Parts of the Solar System
Earth & Space Science	17	Water on Earth
Earth & Space Science	18	Taking Care of Our Planet
Earth & Space Science	19	The Day and Night Sky
Engineering	20	Engineering

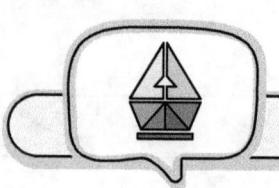
Next Generation Science Standards Correlation Guide

Unit	Week	Next Generation Science Standard	Description of Standard
Physical Science	1	2-PS1-1 2-PS1-2	Describe and classify different types of matter by their observable properties.
Physical Science	2	2-PS1-2	Plan and conduct an investigation to describe and classify different kinds of materials by their observable properties.
Physical Science	3	2-PS1-2	Explore and analyze chemical reactions between two types of matter.
Physical Science	4	2-PS1-2	Describe and classify different types of matter using the characteristics of light.
Physical Science	5	2-PS1-2	Explore how sound travels through different types of matter.
Life Science	6	2-LS4-1	Describe the differences between vertebrates and invertebrates and identify animals that belong in each category.

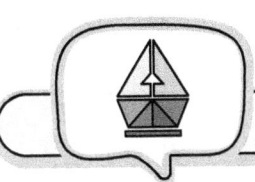
Unit	Week	Next Generation Science Standard	Description of Standard
Life Science	7	2-LS2-1A	Understand and explain the steps of the water cycle.
Life Science	8	2-LS2-1 2-LS2-2	Explain the process of pollination and the importance of pollinators to our ecosystem.
Life Science	9	2-LS2-1 2-LS4-1	Define and describe the different parts of a plant, as well as their individual functions.
Life Science	10	2-LS4-1	Make observations of plants and animals to compare the diversity of life in different habitats.
Life Science	11	2-LS4-1	Explain how adaptations help plants and animals to survive in their environments.
Life Science	12	2-ESS1-1	Describe the importance of the sun and what it provides the Earth.

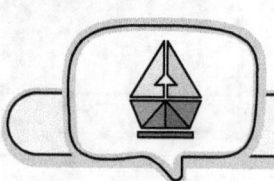
Unit	Week	Next Generation Science Standard	Description of Standard
Earth & Space Science	13	2-ESS1-1 2-ESS2-1	Explain the process of erosion and its impact on the environment.
Earth & Space Science	14	2-ESS1-1	Identify a variety of natural disasters and explain their impact on the environment.
Earth & Space Science	15	2-ESS1-1	Identify the similarities and differences between the four seasons.
Earth & Space Science	16	2-ESS1-1	Identify different parts of the solar system and how they interact with one another.
Earth & Space Science	17	2-ESS2-2 2-ESS2-3	Identify where water is found on Earth and that it can be in solid or liquid form.
Earth & Space Science	18	K-2-ETS1-1 2-ESS1-1	Identify ways in which people can care for the planet.

Unit	Week	Next Generation Science Standard	Description of Standard
Earth & Space Science	19	2-ESS1-1	Understand and explain the phases of the moon, as well as similarities and differences between the day sky and night sky.
Engineering	20	K-2-ETS1-1 K-2-ETS1-2	Gather information to define a simple problem that can be solved through the development of a robot.

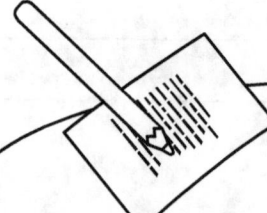

WEEK 1

Physical Science

Classifying Matter Based On Hardness, Weight, Texture and Flexibility

2-PS1-1
2-PS1-2

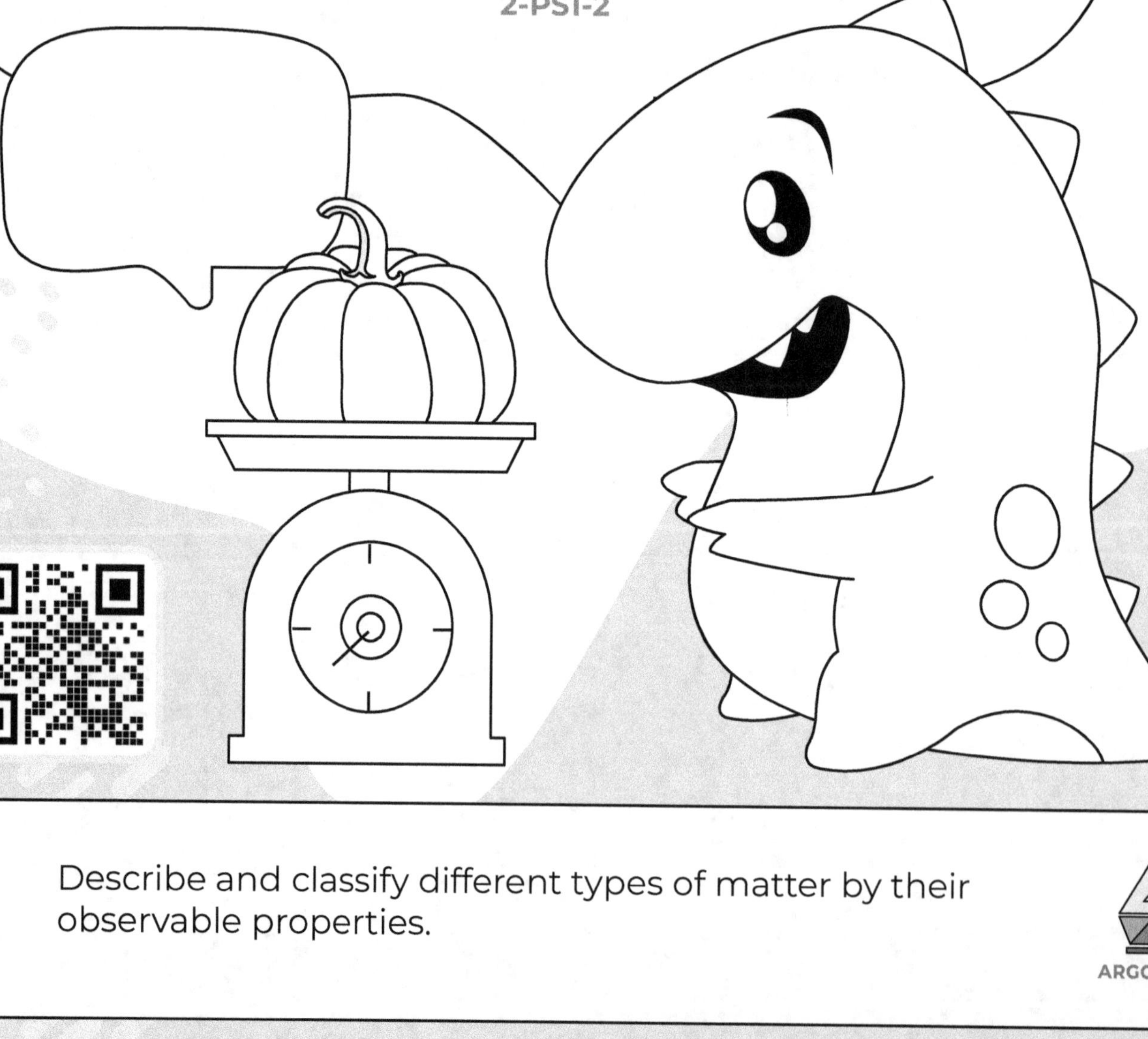

Describe and classify different types of matter by their observable properties.

ARGOPREP

Directions: Read the text below. Then answer the questions that follow.

What is matter?

In science, **matter** is anything that takes up space. Everything you see around you is made of matter - this workbook, your body, the buildings around you. In science, it can be helpful to group different kinds of matter by the characteristics they have. Some characteristics include color, hardness, weight, texture, and flexibility. **Hardness** means how tough an object is. **Weight** is how heavy it is. **Texture** describes how something feels when we touch it, such as rough or squishy. **Flexibility** is how easy it is to bend something without breaking it. We can explore these characteristics by using our senses - looking at the object, feeling the object, holding the object, and seeing if the object makes a sound on a solid surface.

Directions: Read the questions below and choose the best answer for each question.

1. What makes up everything around you and also takes up space?

   A. Color

   B. Matter

   C. Hardness

2. How something feels is a characteristic known as:

   A. Flexibility

   B. Color

   C. Texture

3. How can you explore the characteristics of an object?

   A. By holding it

   B. By looking at it

   C. Both A and B

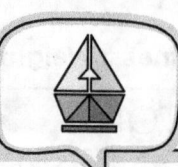
Yesterday, you learned about the characteristics of matter. Today you will focus on exploring the color of matter.

Directions: Today we are going to group matter by color. Next to each color listed below, write 5 items that are that color. Yellow has been done for you as an example.

YELLOW -lemon, sunflower, banana, construction worker's vest

RED

....

BLUE

....

BLACK

....

PURPLE

....

GREEN

....

BROWN

....

WHITE

....

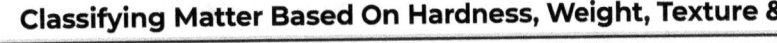
Follow Up Questions:

1. Which color was it easiest to think of objects for?

....

....

....

....

2. Which color is your favorite?

....

....

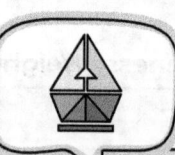
Yesterday, you explored how matter can be classified by color. Today you will explain how the hardness and weight of objects can be very different depending on what types of matter you are observing.

Directions: Collect the items listed below. Then pick up and observe each item. Lastly, list them from hardest and heaviest (the most weight) to softest and lightest (the least weight).

SOFTEST AND LIGHTEST

....

....

....

....

....

....

....

....

....

....

lined white paper

ruler

spoon

crayon

cracker

construction paper

aluminum foil

rubber band

candle

eraser

HARDEST AND HEAVIEST

 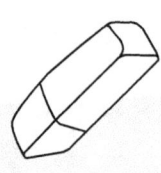 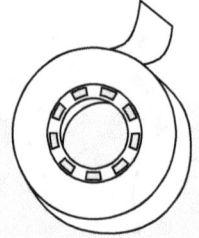 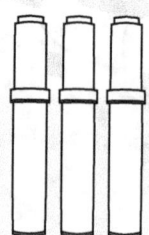 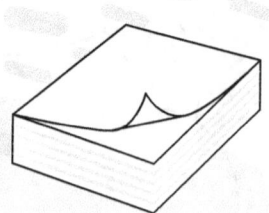

Follow Up Questions:

1. Can an object be hard and weigh very little?

   A. Yes

   B. No

2. Which object was the heaviest?

....

....

3. Can you think of an object that is very soft but also very heavy? List it below.

....

....

....

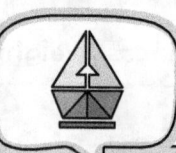
You have spent several days learning about, exploring and explaining how different matter has different characteristics such as weight, hardness and color. Today you will experiment with the different textures that matter can have.

Directions: Texture is the feel or look of an object. You can observe texture with your eyes and hands. In the box below are different types of textures. Walk around your house and feel different objects and matter. Identify objects that have each type of texture and write them in the chart below.

rough	smooth	soft
•	•	• ....
•	•	• ....
•	•	• ....
hard	**bumpy or lumpy**	**gritty**
•	•	• ....
•	•	• ....
•	•	• ....

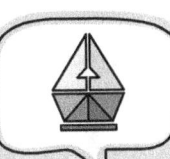
Below is a list of different objects you may have in your home. Describe their textures on the lines. You can use the terms above, as well as other terms you know to describe the object's texture.

1. pillow - ....

....

2. coffee grounds - ....

....

3. cotton ball - ....

....

4. chocolate bar - ....

....

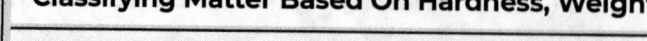
Yesterday, you experimented with determining the textures of different objects. Today you will elaborate on the characteristic of flexibility by testing common objects around your house in order to see whether or not they are flexible.

Directions: Collect the objects listed below from around your house. Play with them, touch them and try to gently bend them without breaking them. If they easily bend without breaking, they are flexible. If they do not easily bend, they are not flexible. Group items based on whether they are flexible or not and write the object's name in the correct column.

Items to collect and categorize:

1. hair tie
2. glass
3. slinky
4. straw
5. granola bar

6. pencil
7. rubber band
8. leaf
9. ruler
10. calculator

FLEXIBLE	NOT FLEXIBLE
•	•
•	•
•	•
•	•
•	•
•	•
•	•
•	•
•	•

WEEK 2

Physical Science

Classifying Matter Based on Strength, Force and Hardness

2-PS1-2

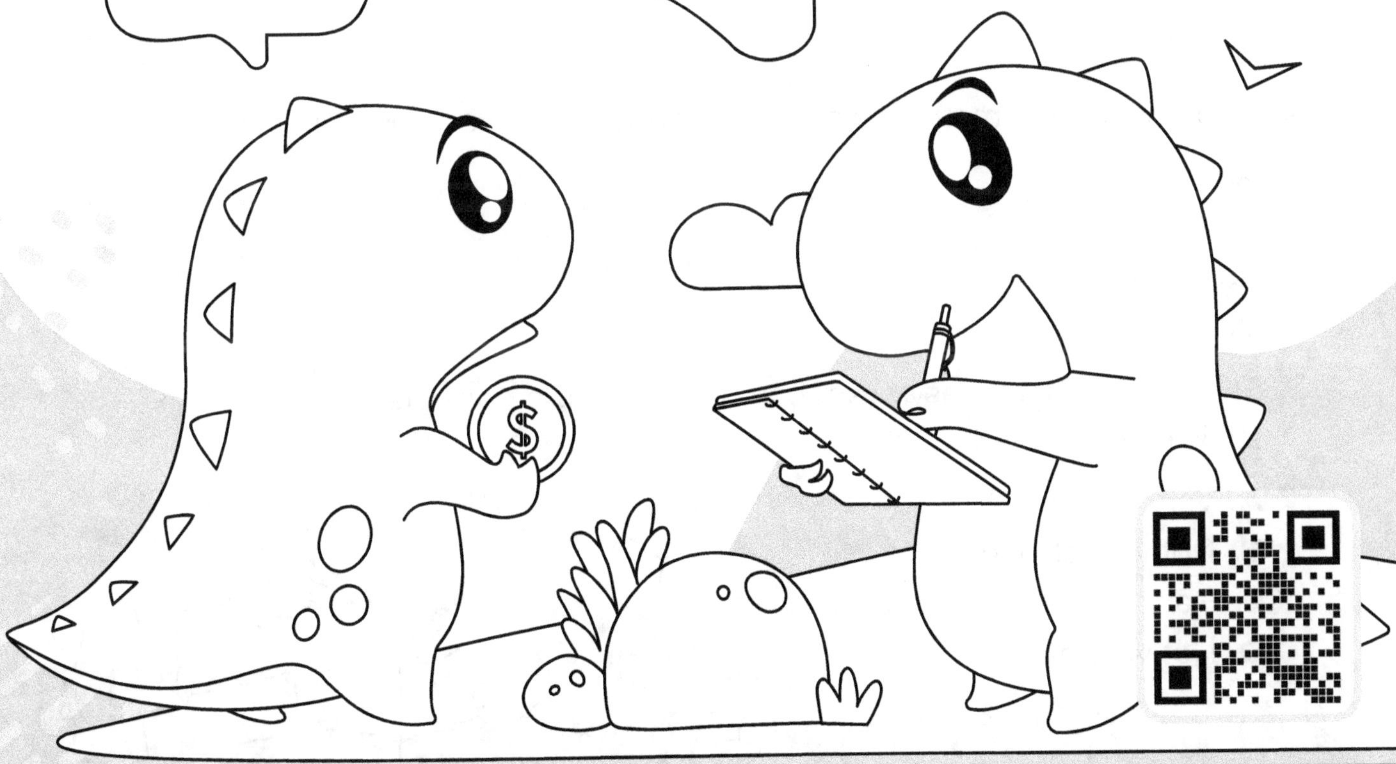

Plan and conduct an investigation to describe and classify different kinds of materials by their observable properties.

Directions: Read the text below. Then answer the questions that follow.

Strength, Force & Hardness

The **strength** of matter determines how easy it is to break or snap something into pieces. Something that is strong is difficult to break; something that is not strong is easy to break. **Force** is a push or a pull used on an object in order to make it move. Some things, such as large boulders, require a lot of force in order to get them to move. Other things, such as marbles, require very little force to get them to move. Sometimes we force an item to move by pushing it or pulling it. Did you know that you can also use force in order to make things move faster or slower or even to stop something from moving? **Hardness** is how tough the surface of something is. We can test how hard something is by how easily it scratches.

1. You can classify the hardness of matter by seeing how easy it is to scratch the surface of it.

   A. True

   B. False

2. If you wanted to move a heavy sofa, you would have to use a lot of ....

   A. Hardness

   B. Strong

   C. Force

   D. Texture

3. Something that is easy to snap in half, such as a popsicle stick, is considered ....

   A. Very strong

   B. Not very strong

   C. Hard

   D. Not very hard

Yesterday, you learned about new characteristics of matter. Today you will focus on exploring the strength of matter around your home.

Directions: Reread the opening sentences from yesterday about strength. Then, follow the directions below to test different items based on their strength and answer the questions that follow.

Materials Needed:

1. 2 similar sized books
2. 10 pennies
3. 1 plastic grocery bag
4. 1 piece of white paper
5. 1 piece of aluminum foil
6. tape

1. Make a prediction. Which material will hold the most pennies? Why?

_____

_____

Space your two books about a hand's length apart. Spread the plastic bag across the books and tape it down. Stack the pennies in between and see how many it can hold.

2. How many pennies did the plastic bag hold?

_____

_____

Repeat the directions above, switching out the plastic bag for the piece of paper and the aluminum foil.

3. How many pennies did the computer paper hold?

_____

4. How many pennies did the aluminum foil hold?

....

Now, let's look at the results!

....

5. Which material held the most pennies? What does that tell you about its strength?

....

....

6. Which material held the least amount of pennies? What does that tell you about its strength?

....

....

7. Look back at your prediction. Were you correct? Explain why or why not.

....

....

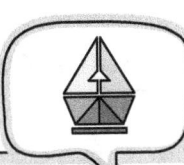
Yesterday, you explored the strength of different materials around your home. Today you will explain how force is related to different household activities and objects.

Directions: Reread the opening sentences from Day 1 about force. Then, read each of the situations below. Explain whether the sentence describes the force of a push or a pull.

1. Mowing the lawn with a standing lawn mower

....

2. Opening dresser drawers to get out clothes

....

3. Playing the game tug of war

....

4. Playing basketball and shooting a basket from the free throw line

....

5. Kicking a soccer ball and making a goal

....

....

....

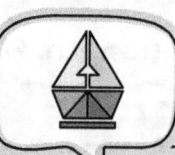
6. Crushing a soda can with your bare hands

....

....

7. Shopping in the grocery store with a shopping cart

....

....

8. Getting the garden hose and moving it to the other end of the house

....

....

9. Putting the chair under the dining room table

....

....

10. A woman walking with a walker

....

....

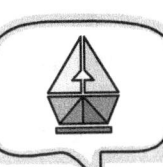
Yesterday, you explored how pushing or pulling an item can force it to move. Today you will experiment further with this idea by considering situations where force is used in everyday activities.

Directions: Read the short passages. Then, answer the questions that follow based on how to change a person's force.

1. Angela is sitting on a lawn chair outside. The soccer ball comes to her. From the chair, Angela kicks the soccer ball to her sister, Erica. The soccer ball did not go far at all. How can Angela make the ball go faster? How should she change her force?

....

....

2. Tyra is riding her bike. She sees a big hill with lots of pebbles. She is worried. She should go slower so she doesn't fall or lose control. How can Tyra go slower? How could she change her force?

....

....

3. Jenna is eating an apple. She drops the apple on the ground from a standing position. She is surprised to see that nothing happened to the apple. Jenna wants to know how much force she has to exert in order to make a dent in the apple. What can she do to make the apple have a dent? What force should she use?

....

....

....

....

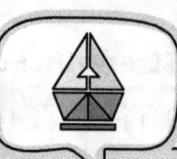
Yesterday, you experimented with different scenarios where force can be used in different ways. Today you will elaborate on the concept of hardness by testing how easy it is to scratch different items.

Directions: Complete the experiment based on testing hardness. Then, answer the questions that follow.

Materials Needed:

1. a penny
2. a paper napkin
3. a paper plate
4. notebook paper
5. a washrag
6. a rock

1. Make a prediction. What item will be the hardest? What item will be the weakest? Explain.

....

For this experiment you will scratch each item with a penny.

2. What happened to the napkin? Was it easy to scratch? Explain.

....

....

3. What happened to the plate? Was it easy to scratch? Explain.

....

....

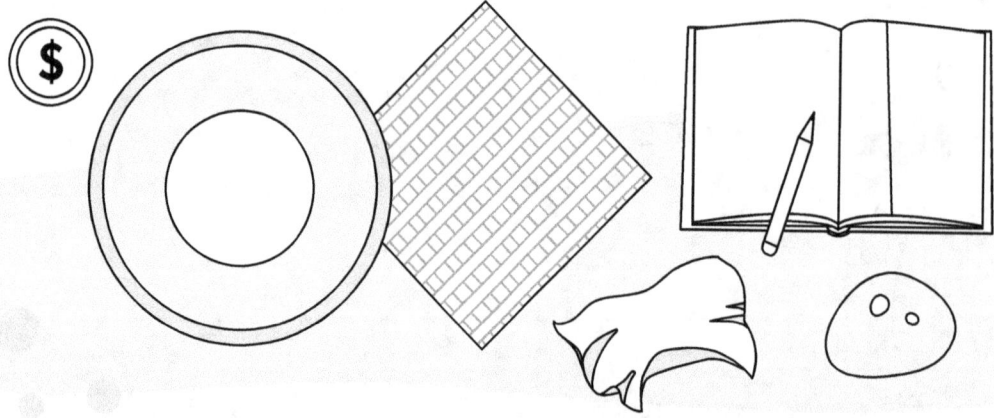

4. What happened to the notebook paper? Was it easy to scratch? Explain.

....

....

5. What happened to the washrag? Was it easy to scratch? Explain.

....

....

6. What happened to the rock? Was it easy to scratch? Explain.

....

....

7. Were you correct in your predictions? Explain.

....

....

WEEK 3

Physical Science

Chemical Reactions and States of Matter

2-PS1-2

Explore and analyze chemical reactions between two types of matter.

ARGOPREP

Directions: Read the text below. Then answer the questions that follow.

States of Matter

All objects on Earth are made up of matter. Matter comes in three different forms-solid, liquid, and gas. **Solids** have a specific shape. That shape does not change. **Liquids** take up space like solids do, however, they do not keep the same shape. The shape of a liquid depends on the container you put it in. The last type of matter is gas. **Gasses** spread out to fill their container, such as a balloon, and they do not have a certain shape.

When different kinds of matter interact, they can create what is known as a **chemical reaction**. Chemical reactions occur when two or more things are mixed together and form a new type of matter. An example of this would be baking a cake. When you mix flour, sugar, eggs and oil together and put them in the oven, you'll have a cake when it is done baking. The cake looks and tastes very different from how any of those ingredients taste on their own. This is because a chemical reaction occurred to produce a brand new type of matter.

1. Which form of matter takes up space but changes shape?

    A. Solid

    B. Liquid

    C. Gas

2. Which form of matter spreads out to fill its container and is not in a specific shape?

    A. Solid

    B. Liquid

    C. Gas

3. When two or more types of matter produce a new type of matter, it is called a:

    A. Chemical reaction

    B. Gas

    C. Solid

    D. Liquid

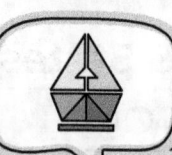
Yesterday, you learned about the different states of matter and chemical reactions. Today you will group materials based on their state of matter.

Directions: Think about the state of matter of each object below when it is at room temperature. Write solid, liquid or gas on the line.

1. Orange juice _____

2. Oxygen _____

3. Shoes _____

4. Hand sanitizer _____

5. Chicken nuggets _____

6. Honey _____

7. Chocolate bar _____

8. Dirt _____

9. Carbon Dioxide _____

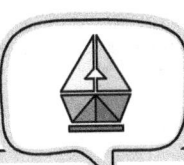
Yesterday, you explored the states of matter that different objects have at room temperature. Today you will explain how the experiment below is an example of a chemical reaction.

Directions: Complete the experiment below. Then, answer the questions that follow.

Materials Needed:

1. empty water bottle
2. baking soda
3. a balloon
4. vinegar
5. a spoon

Begin by putting a spoonful of baking soda into a balloon. Then, fill an empty water bottle halfway up with vinegar. Take the end of the balloon and put it around the top of the water bottle.

1. What is the original state of matter that the baking soda is in?

2. What is the original state of matter that the vinegar is in?

3. What do you think will happen when the baking soda touches the vinegar?

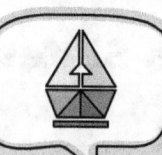

Hold the top of the water bottle where the balloon is and stand the balloon up so the baking soda goes into the bottle.

4. What happened after the baking soda mixed with the vinegar?

....

....

5. How did the state of matter change? Explain what happened to each material.

....

....

vinegar
+
water

Yesterday, you explored the chemical reaction between baking soda and vinegar. Today you will experiment with a different chemical reaction.

Directions: Complete the chemical reaction experiment below. Then, answer the questions that follow.

Materials Needed:

1. cup of water
2. $\frac{1}{2}$ cup of white glue
3. a plastic bowl
4. 2 teaspoons of baking soda
5. a spoon

1. Mix the water and baking soda together. What happens?

....

....

....

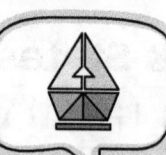
2. Mix the liquid with the glue. What happens?

....

....

....

3. After stirring, what happens to your liquid mixture?

....

....

....

4. How did the state of matter change? Explain what happened to each material.

....

....

....

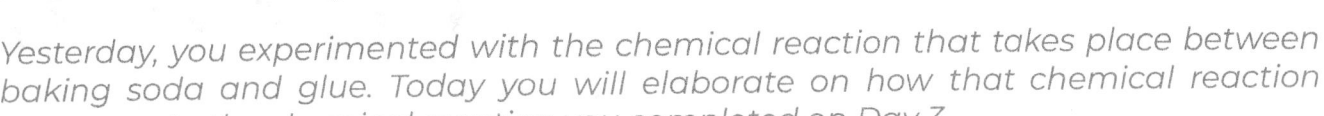
Yesterday, you experimented with the chemical reaction that takes place between baking soda and glue. Today you will elaborate on how that chemical reaction compares to the chemical reaction you completed on Day 3.

Directions: Read and answer the questions below.

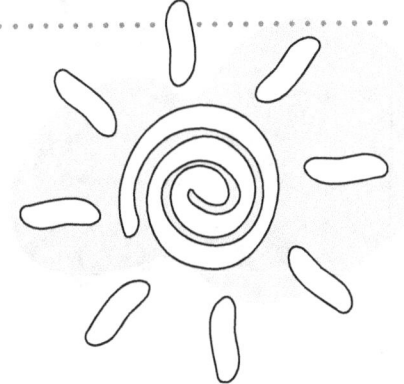

1. Which chemical reaction created bubbles and gas?

   A. Baking soda and vinegar

   B. Baking soda and white glue

2. Which chemical reaction created a thick slimy liquid?

   A. Baking soda and vinegar

   B. Baking soda and white glue

3. Which chemical reaction required you to mix two different states of matter together?

   A. Baking soda and vinegar

   B. Baking soda and white glue

   C. Both

4. Even though baking soda was part of both chemical reactions, the final matter created was very different.

   A. True

   B. False

5. Which reaction did you enjoy the most?

   A. Baking soda and vinegar

   B. Baking soda and white glue

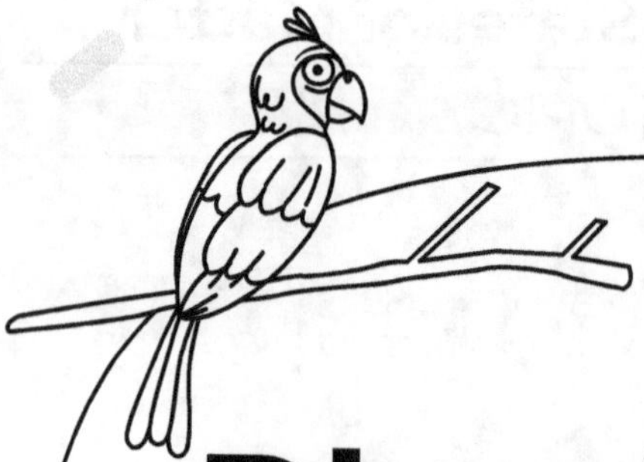

WEEK 4

Physical Science

The Characteristics Of Light

2-PS1-2

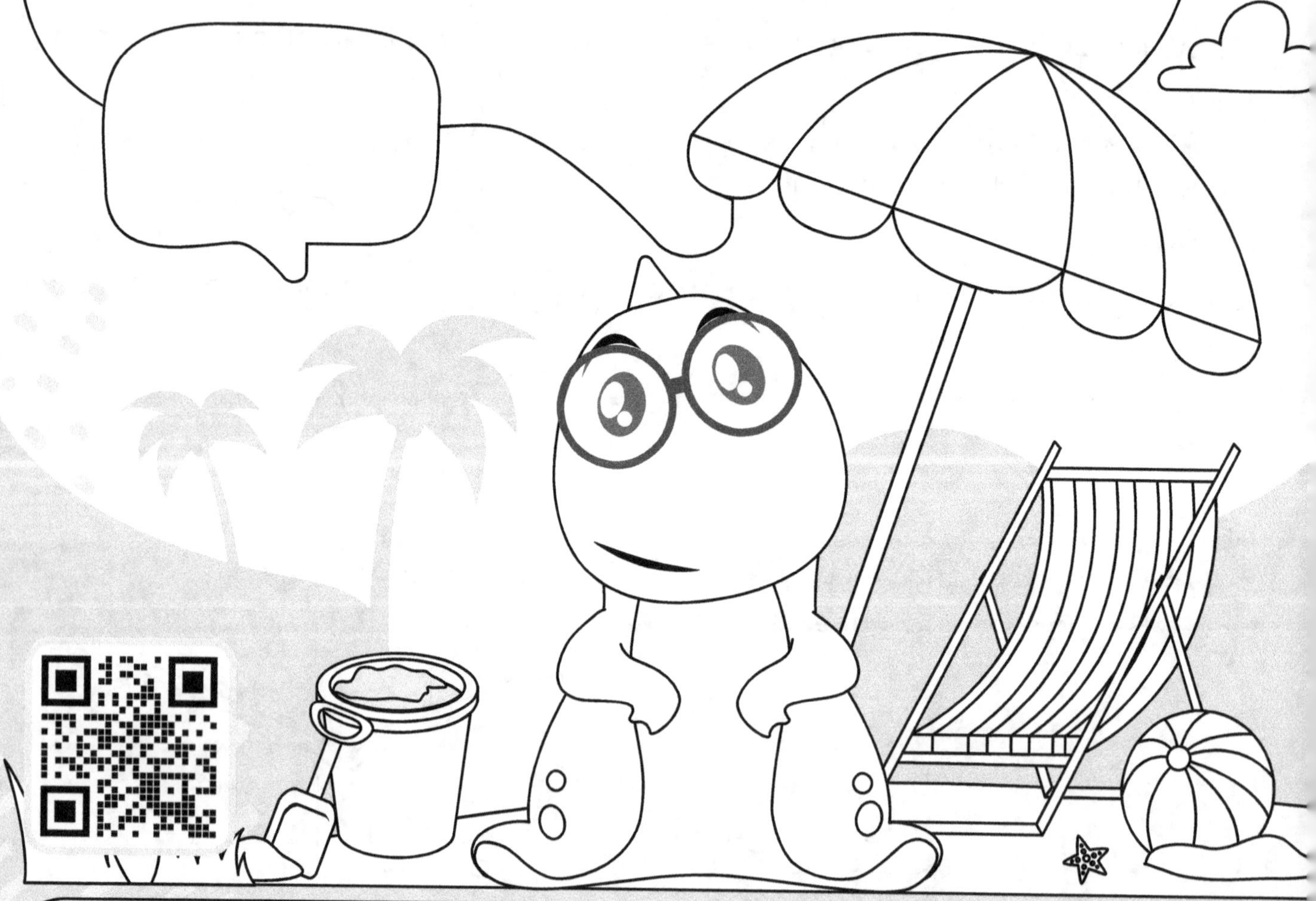

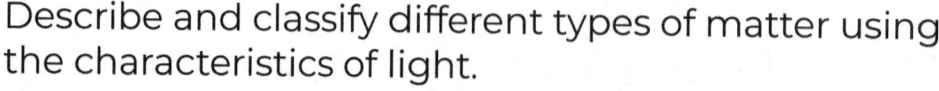

Describe and classify different types of matter using the characteristics of light.

Directions: Read the text below. Then answer the questions that follow.

Light & The Sun

Light is all around us! The word **luminous** describes light. If something is luminous, it means it gives off a lot of light. A major source of light is the sun. Our world would be dark if the sun did not give off light. Plants would not grow because plants get their energy from the sun. If plants do not grow, animals and humans would not be able to eat. The sun also gives off heat which keeps our planet warm.

We often classify matter based on how it interacts with light. For instance, the word **transparent** means that matter allows light to pass through it. A window is transparent because light can be seen easily through it. If something is **opaque** it means that light cannot travel easily through it. A stone wall is opaque because it blocks light and is not see-through.

1. Which of these objects is luminous?

   A. A window

   B. The sun

   C. A wall

   D. A flower

2. A clear crystal ball is opaque.

   A. True

   B. False

3. Which word best describes whether or not light would be able to travel through a glass of water?

   A. Warm

   B. Opaque

   C. Transparent

   D. Luminous

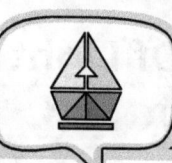
Yesterday, you learned about light, the sun and how light can or cannot travel through different types of matter. Today you will explore transparency and determine what materials in your house are transparent.

Directions: Answer the questions based on an object's transparency.

1. Look around the room you are in. What items in the room are transparent? What items are not transparent? Explain.

....

....

Look at the list of objects below. Identify whether or not each item is transparent. Then explain your reasoning.

2. lamp shade

....

3. window ....

....

4. plastic water bottle ....

....

5. sunglasses ....

....

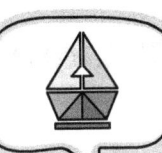
6. curtains ....

....

7. water ....

....

8. textbook ....

....

9. laptop computer ....

....

10. magnifying glass ....

....

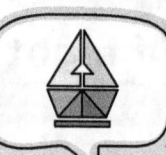
Yesterday, you explored the items in your house that are transparent. Today you will consider a scenario and explain when it would be useful for something to be opaque.

Directions: Read the following scenario and then answer the questions that follow.

Hendrix is making curtains for his room. He has a shade on his window, but it lets some light in around the edges. This is not ideal because light wakes up Hendrix and makes it hard for him to sleep. Hendrix is trying to decide if he should make his curtains out of thin white lace or a thick purple fabric.

1. Think about the colors white and purple. Which color is lighter?

   ....

   ....

2. Think about transparency. Do you think it's easier for light to pass through things that are thick or thin?

   A. Thick

   B. Thin

3. Think about curtains and their job. Curtains are meant to block light. Do you want curtains to be transparent or opaque?

   A. Transparent

   B. Opaque

4. Which material should Hendrix use to make his curtains?

   A. The thin, white lace

   B. The thick, purple fabric

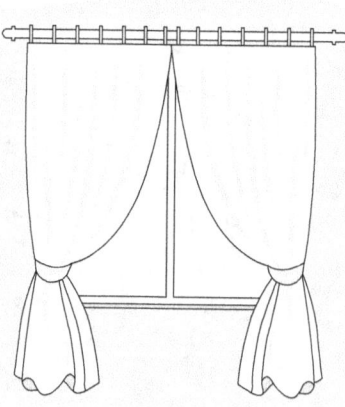

Yesterday, you explored how choosing the right type of opaque fabric can help you make better curtains. Today you will experiment with the warming effects of the sun.

Directions: Complete the activity about the sun's warmth. Then, answer the questions that follow.

Materials Needed:

1. Translucent plastic cups
2. Soil
3. Water
4. Rocks

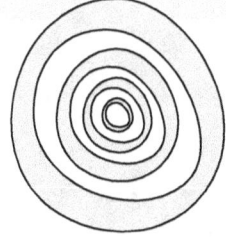

Put each material into a separate cup.

1. Observe the temperature of each item in the cups by holding them in your hands. Explain how they feel on the lines below.

....

....

....

....

Place the cups on a windowsill where they will receive a lot of sunlight. Let them stay there for at least 3 hours.

2. Now that the items have been in the sun, observe the temperature of the cups and the materials inside. Explain how they feel on the lines below.

....

....

....

....

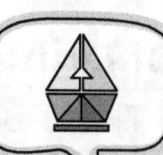
3. What were the differences between the first observations about temperature and the second observations?

....

....

....

....

4. What does this experiment show you about how the sun and heat/warmth are related?

....

....

....

....

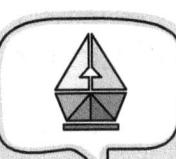
Yesterday, you experimented with how the sun's warmth can change the temperature of objects on Earth. Today you will elaborate on the sun's characteristics and the properties of light.

Directions: For this activity, turn the lights off in the room. Place a piece of aluminum foil over the flashlight and completely cover the front of it. Turn the flashlight on.

Materials Needed:

1. a flashlight
2. aluminum foil
3. a toothpick

1. When you turn the flashlight on, can you see any light coming from the flashlight if it is covered with aluminum foil?

   A. Yes

   B. No

2. Imagine that your flashlight was the sun. What time of day does this remind you of? Explain.

   ....

   ....

   ....

   ....

3. How would you describe the aluminum foil - opaque or transparent?

   A. Opaque

   B. Transparent

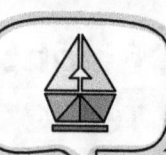
4. Take your toothpick and poke a hole in the aluminum foil. What happens?

....

....

5. Imagine that your flashlight was the sun. Imagine that the aluminum foil represents clouds blocking the sun's light. What do the holes in the aluminum foil represent?

....

....

....

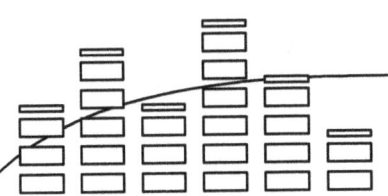

WEEK 5

Physical Science

Sound

2-PS1-2
2-PS1-4

Explore how sound travels through different types of matter.

ARGOPREP

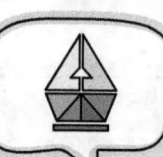
Directions: Read the text below. Then answer the questions that follow.

Sounds Waves

Do you know how sound is made? Sound is made through **vibrations**. The word vibrate means to move quickly. Every sound has a **pitch**, which means how high or low the sound is. For example, a whistle has a high pitch and a bass guitar has a low pitch. Pitch can be changed by how fast or slow the vibration is.

Sound can travel from one place to another. If someone blows a whistle from across a field, you can hear it because the vibrations travel across the field into your ear. Sometimes you can even see sound waves.

1. Can you see sound waves?

   A. Yes

   B. No

2. What does the word vibrate mean?

   A. To move

   B. To move at a fast pace

   C. To run

3. What does the word pitch mean?

   A. The ability to hear sound

   B. How high or low a sound is

   C. How quiet a sound is

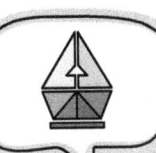
Yesterday, you learned about sound waves and how they are made by vibrations. Today you will explore how sound travels.

Directions: Complete the experiment about how sound travels. Then, answer the questions that follow.

Materials Needed:

1. a plastic baggie puffed up with air
2. a plastic baggie filled with water
3. a pencil
4. a hard surface

1. Tap the pencil on the bag filled with air. Describe the sound.

....

....

2. Tap the pencil on the bag filled with water. Describe the sound.

....

....

3. Tap the pencil on a hard surface like a wall or table. Describe the sound.

....

....

....

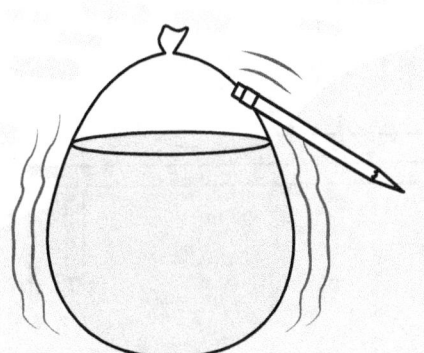

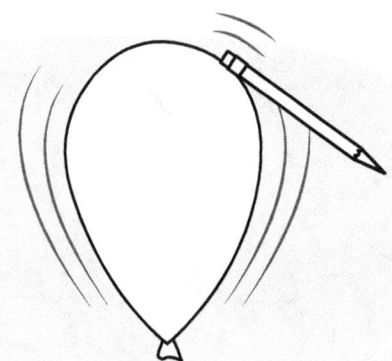

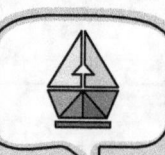
4. How are the sounds different?

....

....

5. Can sound travel through air, water and solid objects? Explain.

....

....

....

Yesterday, you explored how sound can travel through different types of objects, such as water, air and solid plastic. Today you will explain how sound feels based on the types of vibrations you interact with and the speed of vibrations.

Directions: For this activity you will need an electronic device with speakers such as a TV, phone or laptop. Follow the directions step-by-step and answer the questions in order.

1. Turn on the sound on your device. Try to find a song that has the same beat the entire time.

2. Place your hand on or near the speaker. Can you feel the vibration of the music?

   A. Yes

   B. No

3. Turn the volume up so it is louder. Do the vibrations feel more or less intense?

   A. More intense

   B. Less intense

4. Did the pace or speed of the vibrations change when you turned the volume up?

   A. Yes

   B. No

5. Now turn the volume down so it is really quiet. Is it harder to feel the vibrations?

    A. Yes

    B. No

6. Did the pace or speed of the vibrations of the song change when you turned the volume down so that it was quieter?

    A. Yes

    B. No

Yesterday, you explored how volume and vibrations are connected. Today you will experiment with sound by creating a glass xylophone!

Directions: Ask your parent or guardian for permission to use some of the glasses in your house. Choose six glasses that are different sizes and shapes. You will also need a spoon for this activity.

1. Tap each glass with a spoon. Describe the pitch of the sound made when tapping on each glass.

   Glass #1: ....

   Glass #2: ....

   Glass #3: ....

   Glass #4: ....

   Glass #5: ....

   Glass #6: ....

2. Fill the glasses halfway up with water. Repeat the process of tapping the glasses. How does the pitch change when tapping on each glass?

   ....

   ....

   ....

3. Does the material that the glass is made of determine the sound made?

   A. Yes

   B. No

4. How does the water affect the sound that is made?

   ....

   ....

   ....

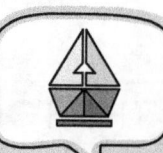
Yesterday, you created your own xylophone out of glasses from around your house. Today you will elaborate on how pitch, vibrations and matter are related.

Directions: Read and answer the following questions.

1. When you tap a glass with more force, is the sound louder or softer?

   A. Louder

   B. Softer

2. Does the speed or pace of the vibrations change when something gets louder?

   A. Yes

   B. No

3. How can you experience sound besides hearing it?

   A. Taste it

   B. Smell it

   C. Feel it

4. What types of matter can sound come from or travel through?

   A. Solid matter like glass

   B. Liquid matter like water

   C. Gas matter like air

   D. All of the above

5. When you tap an empty glass with a spoon, is the pitch high, low or somewhere in between?

WEEK 6

Life Science

Vertebrates and Invertebrates

2-LS4-1

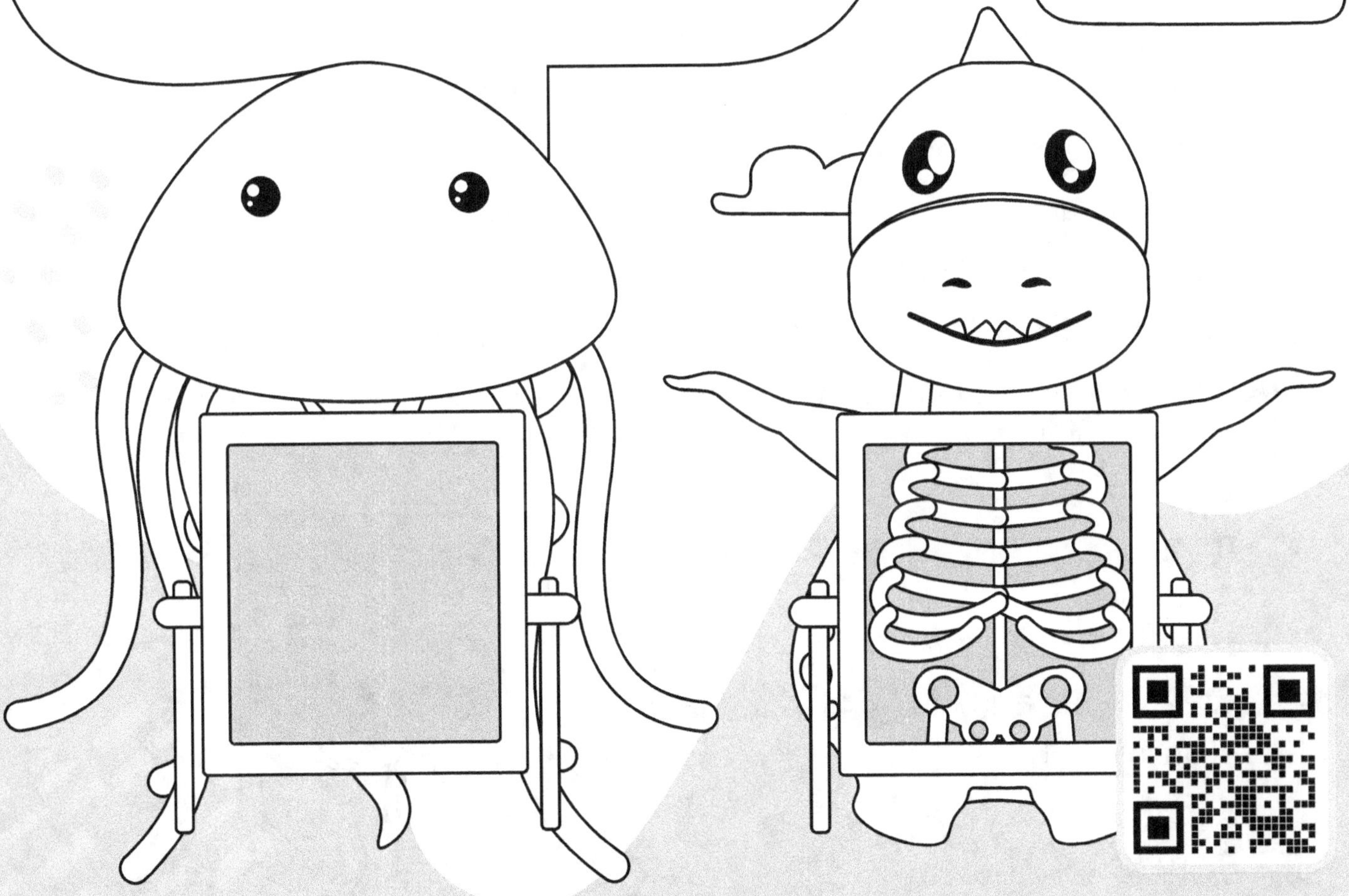

Describe the differences between vertebrates and invertebrates and identify animals that belong in each category.

ARGOPREP

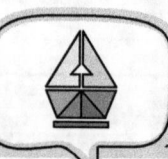
Directions: Read the passage. Then answer the questions that follow.

Vertebrates & Invertebrates

A **vertebrate** is an animal with a backbone. Fish, amphibians, reptiles, birds and mammals are all examples of vertebrates. An **invertebrate** is an animal without a backbone. Worms, mollusks, insects, spiders and crustaceans are examples of invertebrates. Vertebrates and invertebrates can come in all shapes and sizes. In fact, some are so small that they can only be seen through a microscope. Vertebrates and invertebrates can be found in every part of the world. Most of the animals on Earth are invertebrates.

1. An animal without a backbone is called a:

   A. Vertebrate   **B.** Invertebrate

2. An animal with a backbone is called a:

   A. Vertebrate   **B.** Invertebrate

3. Most animals on Earth are:

   A. Vertebrate   **B.** Invertebrate

4. Which of the following is an example of a vertebrate?

   A. Worm
   B. Ant
   C. Lobster
   D. Bear

5. Which of the following is an example of an invertebrate?

   A. Catfish
   B. Turtle
   C. Crab
   D. Lizard

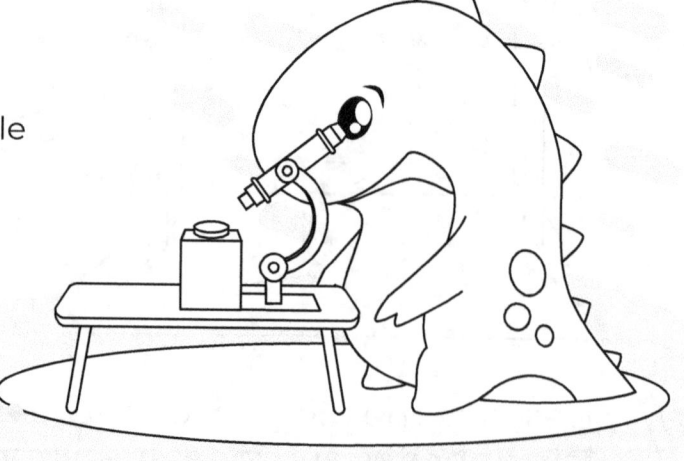

Yesterday, you learned the difference between vertebrates and invertebrates. Today you will explore specific vertebrates and invertebrates.

Directions: Read the list of animals below. Use what you know about vertebrates and invertebrates to sort each animal into the correct category on the next page.

Animals

1. Cardinal

2. Centipede

3. Human

4. Chameleon

5. Lobster

6. Jellyfish

7. Spider

8. Shark

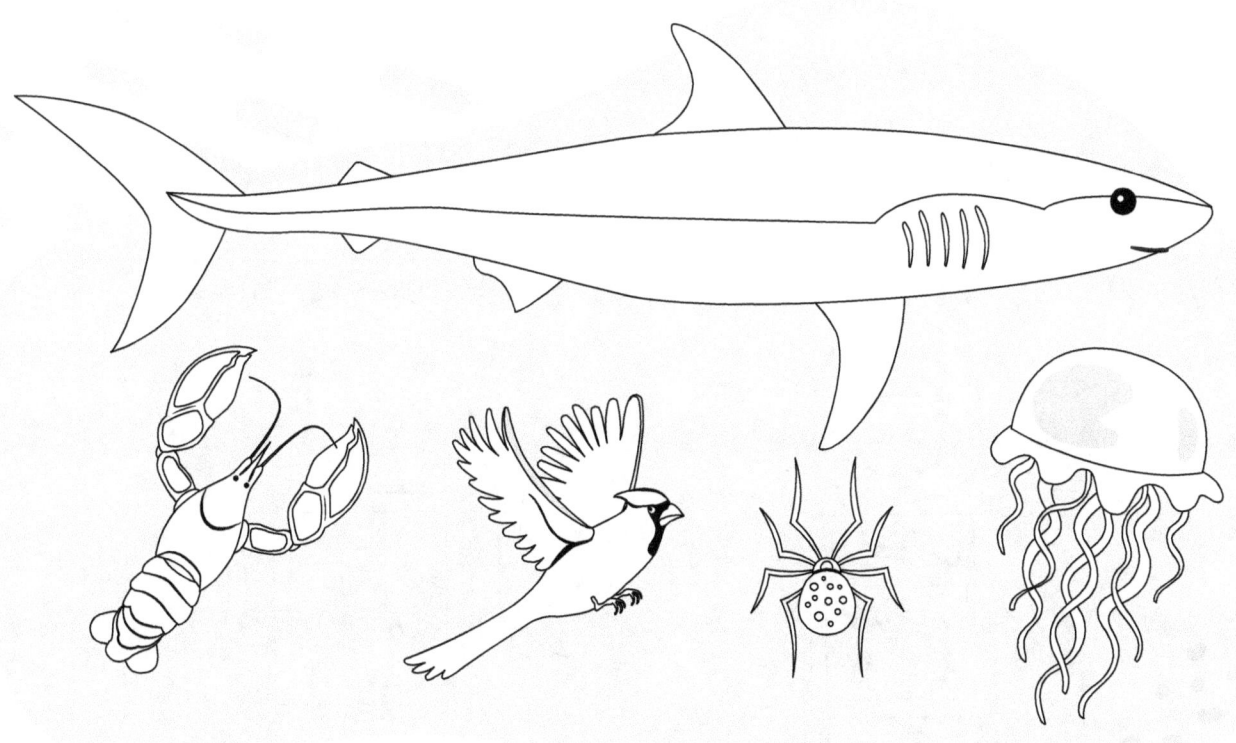

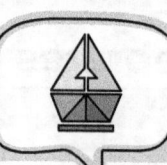
Vertebrate	Invertebrate
....	....
....	....
....	....
....	....
....	....
....	....
....	....
....	....

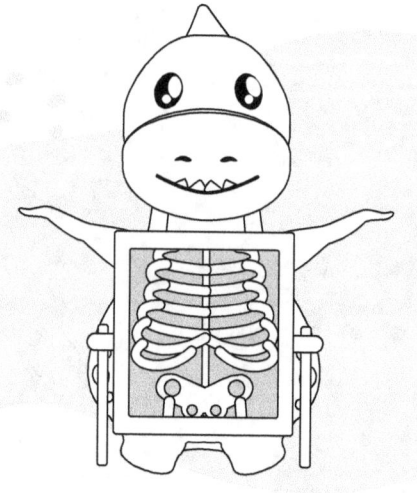
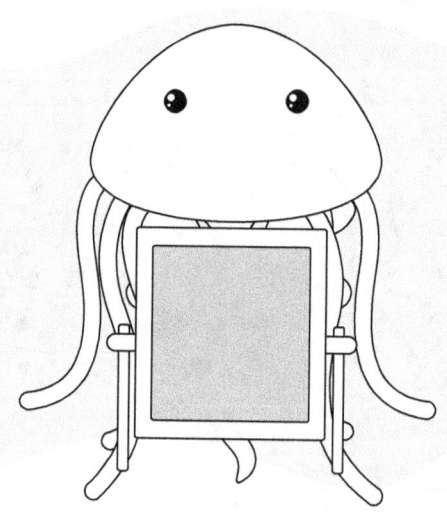

Yesterday, you explored specific vertebrates and invertebrates. Today you will explain key characteristics of a specific invertebrate, the octopus.

Directions: Read the passage. Then answer the questions that follow.

Octopuses

Octopuses are invertebrate sea animals with eight long arms. They live in all oceans on Earth, but they particularly like warm waters. Octopuses usually live deep down in the ocean. They use the suctions found on their arms to pull prey into their mouth.

Larger sea animals such as seals and whales like to eat octopuses. When an octopus feels threatened, it shoots a dark, ink-like substance into the water to confuse its predator. Octopuses are such unique animals!

1. Why are octopuses considered invertebrates?

_____

_____

_____

2. What type of water do octopuses prefer?

_____

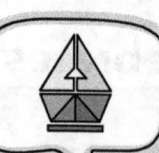
3. Do octopuses usually live in shallow or deep ocean waters?

....

....

....

....

....

4. What do octopuses do when they feel threatened by a predator?

....

....

....

....

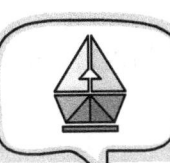
Yesterday, you explained key characteristics of a specific invertebrate - the octopus. Today you will experiment with the different parts of a vertebrate.

Directions: Read the passage and study the picture below.

All vertebrates have several key characteristics, besides a backbone, in common. For instance, every vertebrate also has a brain and bones, no matter how big or small they are. Humans are no different since we are vertebrates.

Directions: Label each of the following parts on the skeleton: the brain, bones and backbone. Be sure to write each of these parts and draw an arrow pointing to that part of the skeleton.

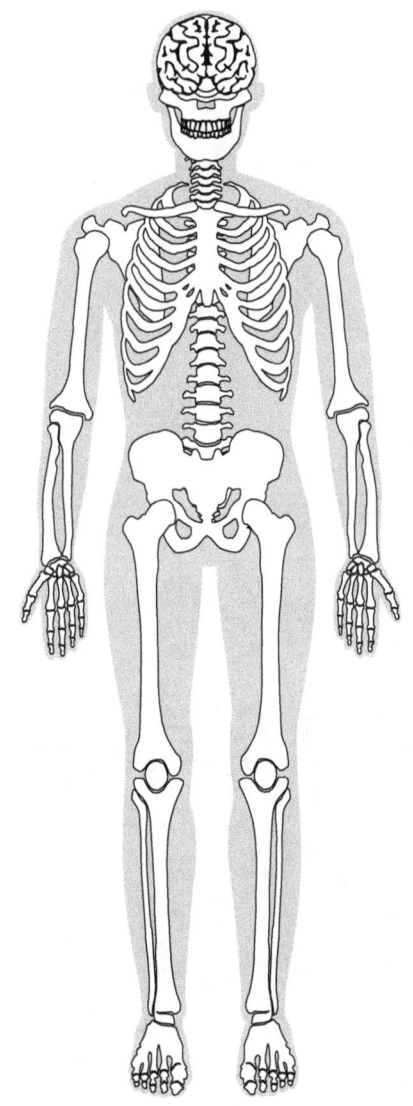

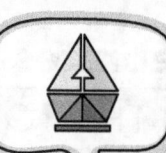
Yesterday, you experimented with identifying the different parts of a vertebrate. Today you will elaborate on this concept by researching and explaining the purpose of each of those parts.

Directions: Complete the table below. Use books or the internet to help you, if necessary.

Vertebrate Part	Job or Function
Backbone	
Bones	
Brain	

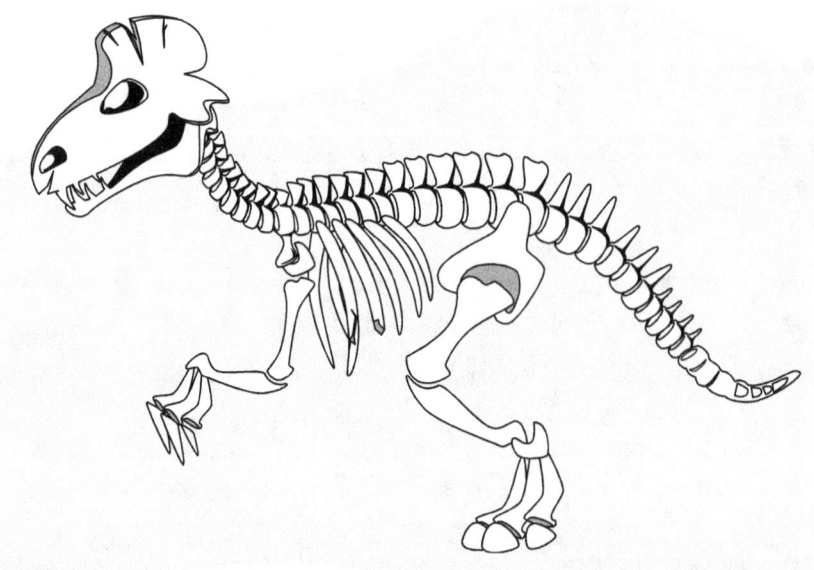

WEEK 7

Life Science

The Water Cycle

2-LS2-1A

Understand and explain the steps in the water cycle.

ARGOPREP

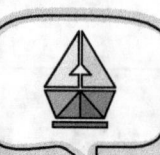
Directions: Read the text below. Then answer the questions that follow.

The Water Cycle

Water is one of the most important types of matter on this planet. Water is used by plants and animals. **The water cycle** helps water move between the Earth and the sky so that it can be used again and again. The water cycle starts with a process called **precipitation**, or rain and snow that falls from the sky. The water soaks into the ground and then makes its way to bodies of water like rivers, lakes, and oceans. When the weather clears up, the sun comes out and heats up the water. This process is called **evaporation**. The water goes back up into the air. When the water cools down, it becomes clouds in a process known as **condensation**. The cycle will then repeat itself when the clouds release precipitation back to Earth.

1. How would you describe the movement of water back and forth between the sky and Earth?

   A. One way

   B. Upward

   C. Downward

   D. A cycle

2. What is it called when water cools down in the sky and forms clouds?

   A. Evaporation

   B. Precipitation

   C. Water Cycle

   D. Condensation

3. What is another name for rain and snow?

   A. Evaporation

   B. Precipitation

   C. Water Cycle

   D. Condensation

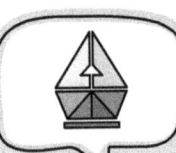
Yesterday, you learned about the different steps in the water cycle. Today you will fill in the diagram below with those steps.

Directions: Look at the diagram below. Fill in the blank spaces with the following phrases that you learned during yesterday's lesson:

- Evaporation
- Precipitation
- Clouds
- The Water Cycle
- Condensation
- Snow
- Lake

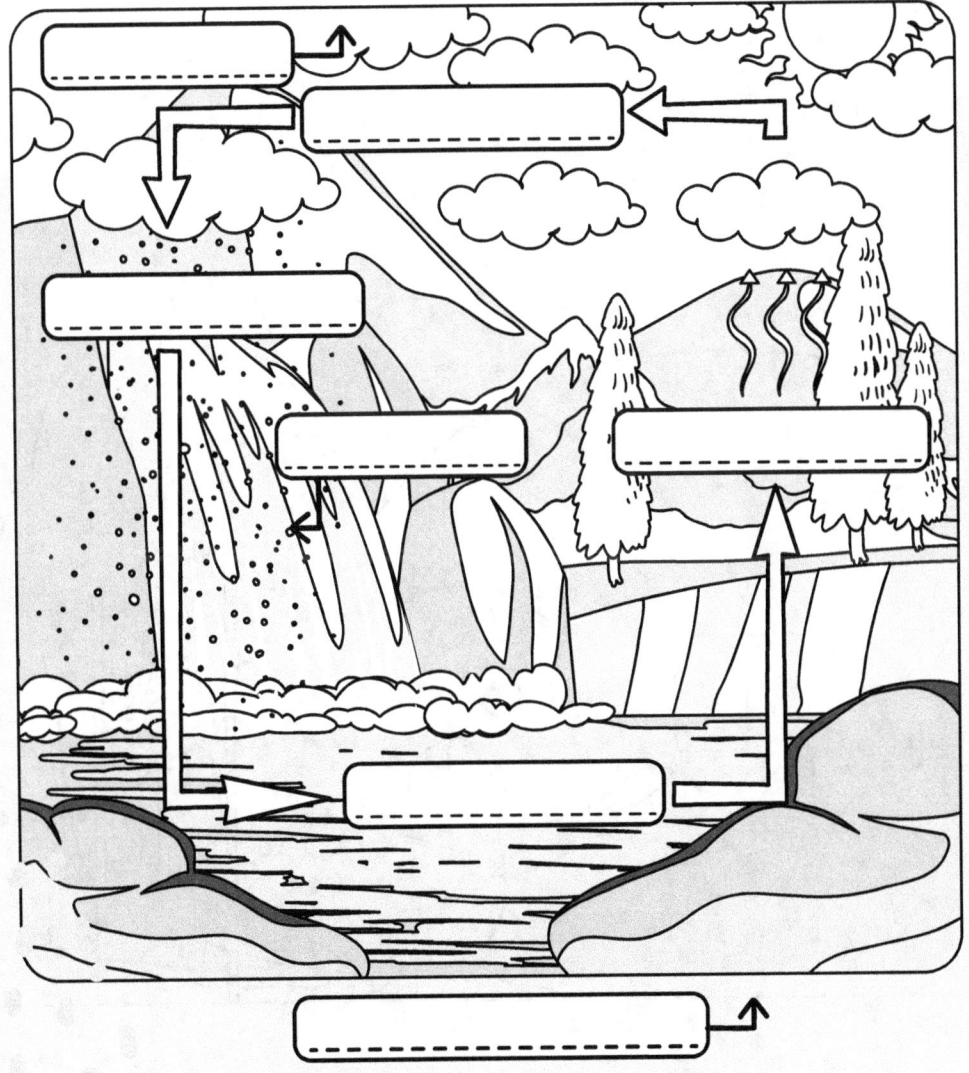

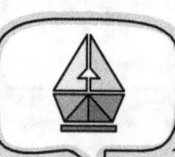
Yesterday, you explored your understanding of the steps of the water cycle. Today you will explain how different demonstrations mimic different parts of the water cycle.

Directions: Complete each of the activities and then answer the questions that follow.

Hose Showers

Go outside and ask your parents to use your hose. Place your finger over the top of it and spray it into the air. Notice how the water falls back to Earth in small droplets.

1. Which step of the water cycle does this represent?

   A. Evaporation

   B. Precipitation

   C. Clouds

   D. Condensation

Cloud In A Pot

Ask your parents to boil a pot of water for you. Once it begins to boil, ask them to take it off the heat and place a clear glass lid or plate on top of the pot. Notice the cloud that begins to form on the lid as the water cools down.

2. Which step of the water cycle does the steam coming from the pot represent?

A. Evaporation

B. Precipitation

C. Snow

D. Condensation

3. Which step of the water cycle does the cooling of the water and the forming of the cloud represent?

A. Evaporation

B. Precipitation

C. Snow

D. Condensation

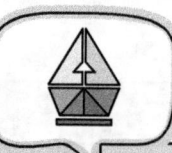
Yesterday, you explored how different activities represent different steps of the water cycle. Today you will experiment with the ideas of flooding and drought.

Directions: Read the passage below. Then, answer the questions that follow.

Precipitation is needed in our world. It provides water to the Earth and helps plants grow. However, too much rain can be a big problem. **Flooding** happens when an area gets too much water, causing the plants to drown and eventually die. The opposite is a problem as well. The word **drought** means there is not enough precipitation in the area. A lack of water makes the ground very dry and plants will eventually die.

1. What does the word drought mean?

....

....

2. Name some places where you think droughts may occur. Use the internet with the help of a parent or guardian to look for places that do not get much rain.

....

....

3. What does the word flood mean?

....

....

4. Name some places where you think floods may occur. Use the internet with the help of a parent or guardian to look for places that get a lot of rain or experience what are called monsoons.

....

....

5. Think about where you live. Is drought or flooding a problem in your community? Explain.

....

....

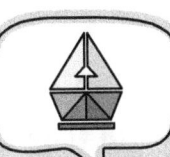
Yesterday, you experimented with the idea of drought and flooding. Today you will elaborate on these events related to the water cycle.

Directions: Read and answer the following questions.

1. When there is a flood, there is too much .... in an area.

    A. Condensation

    B. Precipitation

    C. Sun

    D. Drought

2. Do you think a desert area, an area that does not get much rain, has a lot of evaporation happening in it or not much? Explain why.

....

....

....

....

3. If there were a lot of clouds above your town, what might you experience in the near future? Circle all correct answers.

    A. Drought

    B. Rain

    C. Snow

    D. Condensation

WEEK 8

Life Science
Plants and Pollinators

2-LS2-1
2-LS2-2

Explain the process of pollination and the importance of pollinators to our ecosystem.

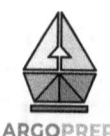

ARGOPREP

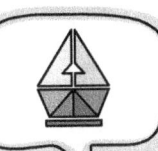
Directions: Read the text below. Then answer the questions that follow.

> Plants, flowers, and trees disperse their seeds. **Disperse** means to spread out. If plants do not disperse their seeds, more plants cannot grow. Seed dispersal is important for plants, flowers, and trees so that they do not crowd one another.
>
> Seeds are dispersed by either wind or **pollinators**. A dandelion makes white, fluffy blossoms. These blossoms have seeds on them. On a windy day, the dandelion seeds can travel hundreds of miles. The reason seeds can travel far is because they need room and space to grow.
>
> Animals and insects known as pollinators can also help disperse seeds. Bees, dragonflies, birds, hummingbirds, and bats are examples of pollinators.

1. What is it called when seeds are spread out?

   A. Dispersal

   B. Pollination

   C. Growth

   D. Crowded

2. Seeds cannot be dispersed by wind.

   A. True

   B. False

3. Which of the following is an example of a pollinator? Circle all correct answers.

   A. Wind

   B. Animals

   C. Bees

   D. Insects

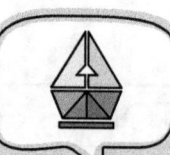
Yesterday, you learned about seed dispersal and pollinators. Today you will explore the resources that plants need and how they get these resources.

Directions: Complete the chart below about how plants get what they need. Ask a parent or guardian to help you use books or the internet to research.

Plants Need:	How Do They Get This?
Carbon Dioxide	
Water	
Light	
Nutrients	

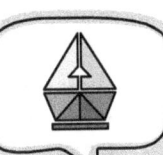
Yesterday, you explored what plants need to survive and how they get those resources. Today you will explain the importance of these resources.

Directions: Answer the questions that follow. Use your research from yesterday to help you.

1. Where do plants get carbon dioxide?

   A. Water

   B. Other plants

   C. Air

   D. Dirt

2. Which of these is a nutrient that a plant uses to grow?

   A. Dirt

   B. Bugs

   C. Nitrogen

   D. Sunlight

3. Why do plants need sunlight?

   A. To disperse

   B. To grow

   C. To pollinate

   D. To breathe

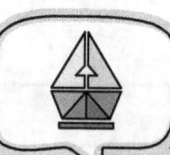
Yesterday, you explained how plants get the things they need. Today you will experiment with a demonstration that illustrates seed dispersal.

Directions: Complete the seed dispersal activity. Then, answer the questions that follow.

Materials Needed:

1. a balloon
2. bird seed
3. a cup
4. a pencil.

1. What do you think you will use to create a seed pod, or a structure that holds lots of little seeds?

....

....

....

2. Make your seed pod by putting the seed in a balloon. Then, blow up the balloon. Blowing up the balloon creates **tension**. What do you think tension means?

....

....

....

3. Tie the balloon. Then, take your pencil and pop the balloon. When you pop the balloon, what happens?

....

....

....

....

4. What does this activity show you about seed dispersal?

....

....

....

....

5. Do you think that the wind could help with the dispersal of a seed pod?

....

....

....

....

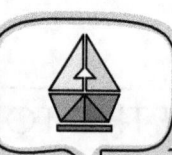
Yesterday, you experimented by modeling seed dispersal. Today you will learn about pollinators.

Directions: Read the passage below. Then, fill in the chart below.

> Bees and wasps have many things in common. They are both insects. They both fly. They both sting. These similarities are why they often are mistaken for each other.
>
> However, even though they are very similar, they do have some important differences. The body of a bee is round and the body of a wasp is long. Bees are hairier than wasps. Bees have flat, little legs that help them collect pollen from flowers. A wasp also has legs, but they are cone shaped. Wasps do not collect a lot of pollen like bees do.
>
> Do both bees and wasps sting? Yes, they both sting; however, bees do not like people. They avoid people whenever they can because they are too busy working. They want to get pollen. They have no interest in harming people. Wasps are different from bees. Wasps are meaner than bees. If they see people, they will want to sting them.

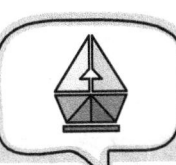
Directions: On the chart below, write the similarities and the differences between bees and wasps.

SIMILARITIES BETWEEN BEES AND WASPS	DIFFERENCES BETWEEN BEES AND WASPS

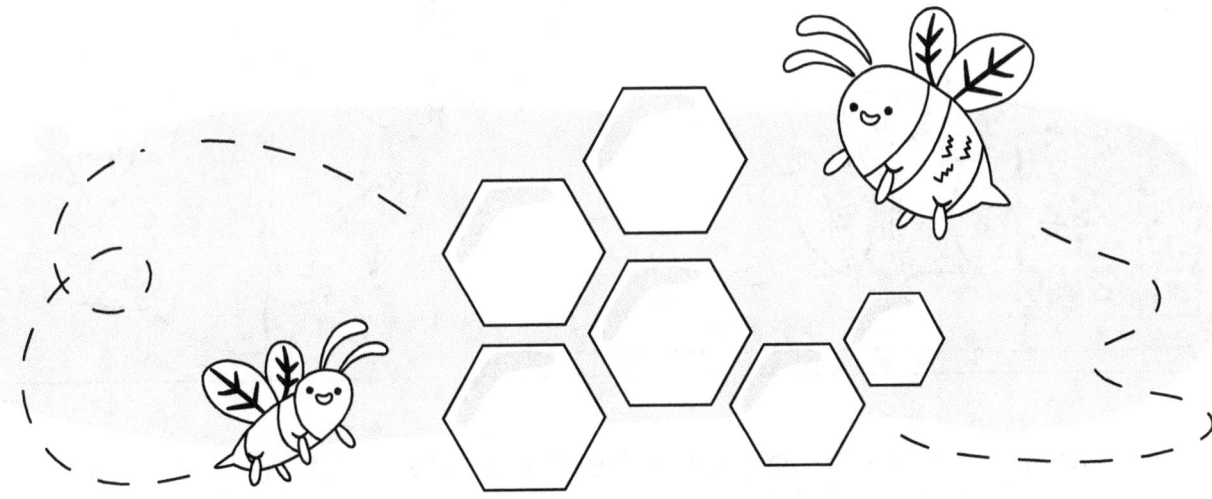

WEEK 9

Life Science

Plants Structures and Functions

2-LS2-1
2-LS4-1

Define and describe the different parts of a plant, as well as their individual functions.

ARGOPREP

Directions: Read the text below. Then answer the questions that follow.

Many things have to happen for a plant to grow. The first thing that happens is a seed **germinates**, or starts to break open. When this happens, the roots push down into the soil to find water. The roots keep the plant grounded and strong. The next step is the growing of the **stem**. The stem grows upwards in order to find light. Plants then grow **leaves**. The leaves take in sunlight in order to make food through the process of **photosynthesis**. As long as the plant continues to get oxygen, sunlight and water, it will thrive and grow.

1. Which part of the plant takes in water?

   A. Roots

   B. Stem

   C. Leaves

2. Which part of the plant is responsible for keeping it in place?

   A. Roots

   B. Stem

   C. Leaves

3. Which part of the plant is responsible for photosynthesis?

   A. Roots

   B. Stem

   C. Leaves

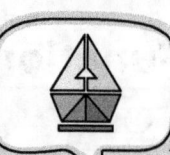
Yesterday, you learned about plant structures and their functions. Today you will explore plant structure by drawing a plant and its parts.

Directions: In the space below, draw a plant. Pick a plant that you think is interesting or beautiful. You can look up a picture of it on the internet or go outside and find one! Label its three main parts: the roots, the stem, and the leaves.

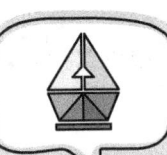
Yesterday, you explored the structures of plants by drawing one of your own! Today you will explain these structures in more detail.

Directions: Go outside and find <u>three</u> different plants. Try to find plants of different shapes and sizes. Look at all of their structures. To observe the roots of the plant, very gently dig around the stem, but do not dig up the whole plant. Then answer the questions below.

1. Do all of the plants you looked at have leaves?

   A. Yes

   B. No

2. What process do you think all of these plants complete with their leaves?

   ....

   ....

   ....

3. What is the job of the roots of these plants?

   ....

   ....

   ....

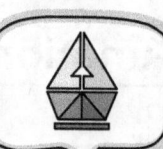

4. Think about the biggest plant you saw. What did you notice was different about the roots of this plant?

....

....

....

5. Do all stems look the same on the plants? Why or why not?

....

....

....

Plants Structures & Functions

EXPERIMENTING WITH THE TOPIC

Yesterday, you explained some of the similarities and differences you noticed between various plants. Today you will explore the different leaves of plants near your home.

Directions: With a parent or guardian, go for a nature walk around your house. Collect five different kinds of leaves. With the help of your parents or guardian, use the Internet to identify the different types of leaves you have collected. On the chart, write down the types of leaves you collected. Then, write down facts about that particular type of tree.

Type Of Tree	Interesting Facts

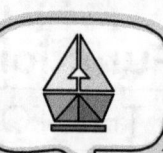
When you have finished, trace the leaves you collected in the space below. Then, color them in and add any additional details you notice.

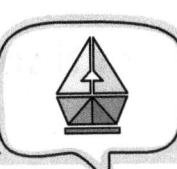
Yesterday, you experimented by collecting and identifying different leaves in your neighborhood. Today you will elaborate on this activity.

Directions: Answer the following questions.

1. Which leaf was your favorite and why? Draw a picture of it below.

....

....

2. What is the most interesting fact you learned about a plant you identified yesterday?

....

....

....

....

3. Of the plants you identified, which one was the smallest?

....

....

....

....

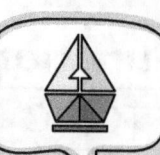
4. What is the function of plant stems?

....

....

....

....

5. What is the function of plant leaves?

....

....

....

....

WEEK 10

Life Science

Habitats

2-LS4-1

Make observations of plants and animals to compare the diversity of life in different habitats.

ARGOPREP

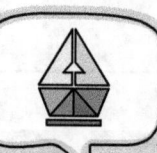
Directions: Read the text below. Then answer the questions that follow.

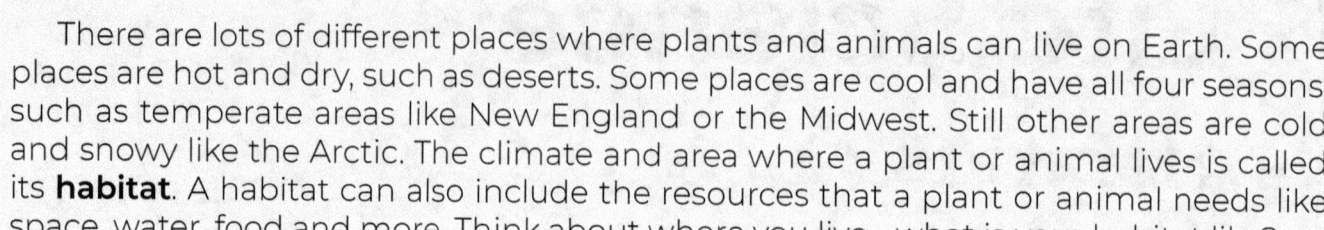

> There are lots of different places where plants and animals can live on Earth. Some places are hot and dry, such as deserts. Some places are cool and have all four seasons, such as temperate areas like New England or the Midwest. Still other areas are cold and snowy like the Arctic. The climate and area where a plant or animal lives is called its **habitat**. A habitat can also include the resources that a plant or animal needs like space, water, food and more. Think about where you live - what is your habitat like?

1. How would you describe a habitat in a temperate area?

   A. Cold and snowy

   B. Hot and dry

   C. Wet and humid

   D. Cool and has four seasons

2. The place where a plant or animal lives is called a ....

   A. Home

   B. Habitat

   C. Desert

   D. Space

3. What resources can be found in any habitat? Choose all correct answers.

   A. Water

   B. Money

   C. Food

   D. Space

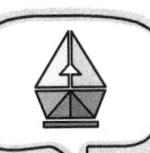
Yesterday, you learned about plant and animal habitats. Today you will explore a particular habitat and answer questions about the plants and animals that live there.

Directions: Answer the questions that follow about a mystery habitat. See if you can guess the habitat described.

1. The temperature here is extremely hot, but you will not need a bathing suit because there is no water. In fact, it is very dry here. What habitat am I?

....

....

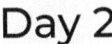

2. What animals and plants live in this kind of habitat?

....

....

Now, imagine you are in a habitat with many trees.

3. What animals might live in this habitat? ....

....

....

4. How do the trees help the animals in this habitat?

....

....

Now, imagine you are in a large grassy habitat.

5. What animals might live in this habitat? ....

....

....

....

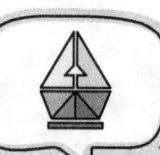
Yesterday, you explored different habitats in more detail. Today you will explain how different habitats provide for different animals.

Directions: Answer the questions that follow about different animals' habitats.

Imagine you are in a water habitat near a lake or a river.

1. What animals live in this particular habitat?

....

....

....

2. Where would animals hide in this type of habitat?

....

....

....

3. What are some predators for water creatures in this habitat?

....

....

....

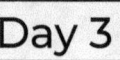

Now, imagine you are in a garden habitat.

4. What animals live in this particular habitat?

....

....

....

5. What do the animals in this habitat eat?

....

....

....

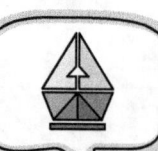

Yesterday, you continued to explain the differences between various habitats. Today you will read about the different plants that are found in different habitats.

Directions: Read the passage below. Then, match the habitats to the correct description.

"

In a **grassland** habitat, there are tall grasses. There are some trees, but usually they are shorter and smaller. There are not many sources of water here.

Desert habitats do not have much vegetation. There is a lot of sand. The plants that grow well in this habitat are cacti and other plants that do not need a lot of water.

Mountain habitats are rocky. There are pine and evergreen trees. The higher up the mountain you travel, the fewer trees you see. Moss grows at the top of the mountain.

Temperate forests have many different kinds of trees.

Freshwater habitats have freshwater, trees, grasses and reeds. The ground is very moist.

The **rainforest** habitat has a very wet ground. There are many tall trees including kapook and tropical trees.

"

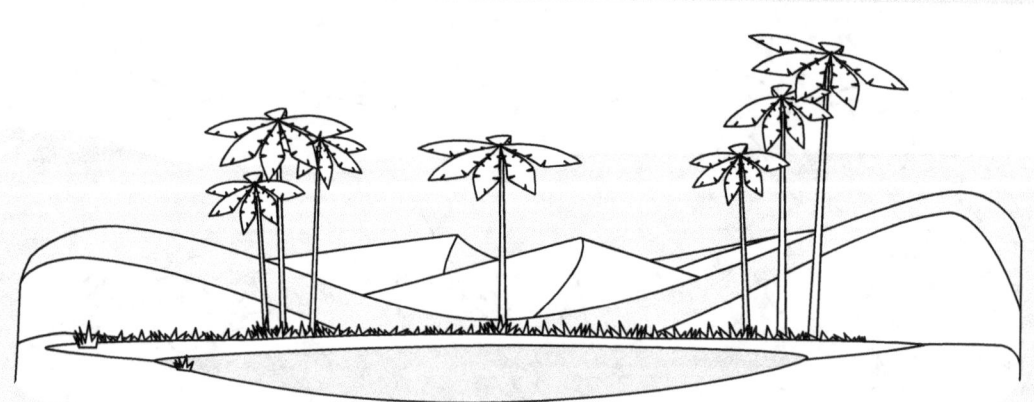

1. Has many tall trees   A. Rainforest

2. No trees no water   B. Freshwater

3. Has many reeds and grasses   C. Temperate Forest

4. Lots of grass and no trees   D. Mountain

5. Has many trees with leaves and needles   E. Desert

6. A rocky habitat with moss   F. Grassland

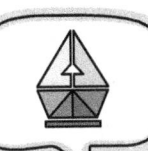
Yesterday, you learned about the plants that are found in various habitats. Today you will elaborate on how animals live in habitats that fit their resource needs.

Directions: Answer the questions that follow based on an animal's need.

1. Where do polar bears live?

....

....

2. What other animals live in this habitat?

....

....

....

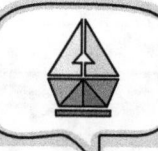
3. What is the weather like in this habitat?

....

....

....

4. Where do sharks live?

....

....

....

5. What other animals live in this habitat?

....

....

....

6. What if sharks would move to where pond frogs live? What would happen?

....

....

....

WEEK 11

Life Science

Adaptation and Survival

2-LS4-1

 Explain how adaptations help plants and animals survive in their environments.

ARGOPREP

Directions: Read the text below. Then answer the questions that follow.

What Is An Adaptation?

The word **adaptation** refers to a trait that helps animals and plants change to survive in their habitat. Over time, plants and animals will change very slowly. For instance, animals have gained adaptations such as fur, different muscles, and new bones to help them better adapt and survive in their environments. Plants have adapted to grow things like thorns and spines for protection against animals who want to eat them. Can you think of any other useful adaptations?

1. Which of the following best describes an adaptation?

   A. A thorn

   B. A habitat

   C. Protection

   D. A trait

2. Fur is a type of adaptation.

   A. True

   B. False

3. What type of adaptation have plants developed over time for their protection?

   A. Leaves

   B. Roots

   C. Thorns

   D. Stems

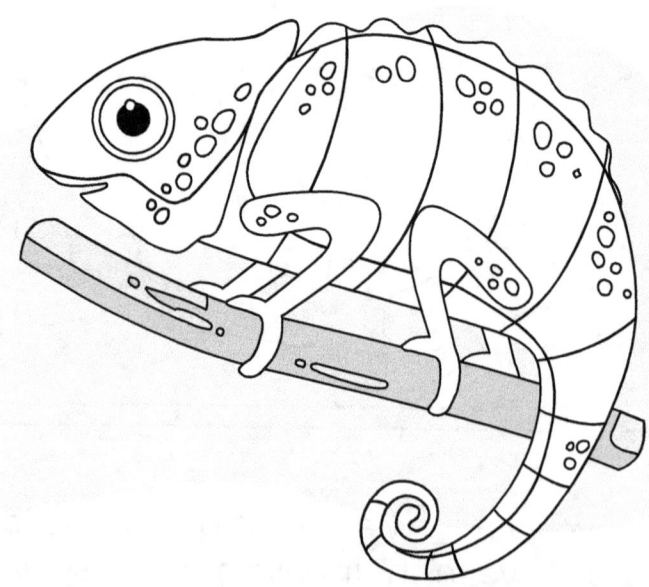

Yesterday, you learned about adaptations that help plants and animals survive in different habitats. Today you will explore specific adaptations in animals.

Directions: On the lines provided, write the name of an animal that uses the adaptation described to survive.

1. Beaks to hold food - ....

2. Sharp claws and feet to dig holes - ....

3. Sharp teeth to help tear and eat food - ....

4. Webbed feet to help swim through water - ....

5. Strong legs for running - ....

6. Which adaptation will help animals eat?

   A. Claws

   B. Wings

   C. Sharp teeth

7. Which adaptation will help animals hide?

   A. Camouflage

   B. Wings

   C. Thick fur

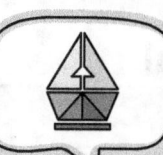
Yesterday, you explored some interesting adaptations that animals have. Today you will explain how different animals use the adaptation of camouflage in order to survive in different habitats.

Directions: Answer the following questions based on how animals camouflage in their environment.

> The word **camouflage** means to disguise or to blend in. Animals use camouflage in their environments all the time. They do this to be safe and to hide from **predators** or animals that want to eat them.

Below is a list of animals and insects to research. Explain how their bodies camouflage into their surroundings. Use the internet to help you.

1. Katydid - ....

....

2. Leopard - ....

....

3. Polar bear - ....

....

4. Coral snake - ....

....

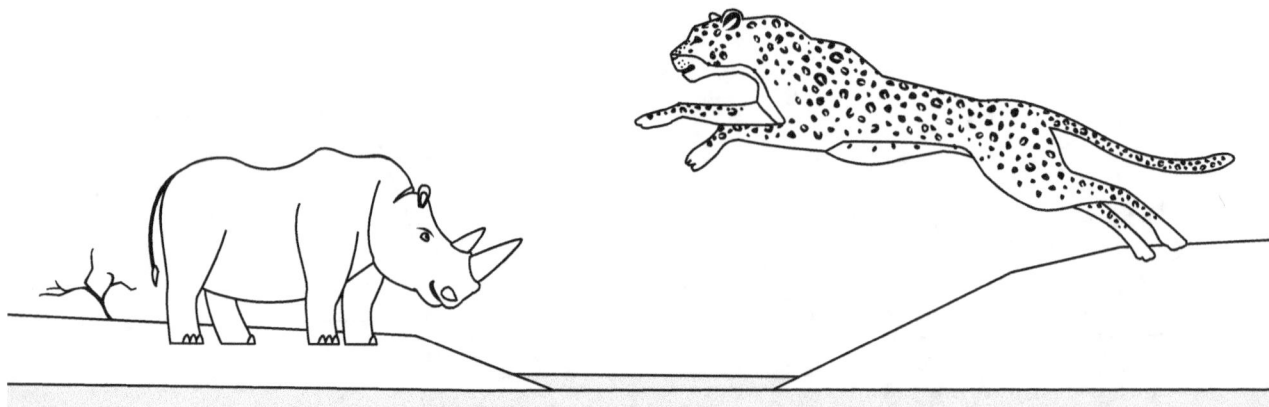

5. Owl - ....

....

6. Moth - ....

....

7. Chameleon - ....

....

8. Walking Stick - ....

....

9. Frogs - ....

....

10. Turtles - ....

....

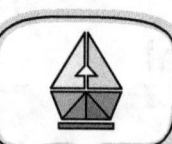
Yesterday you explained how different animals camouflage. Today you will experiment with the idea of animals surviving in their habitats using different adaptations.

Directions: Read the sentences below. Match each animal adaptation to the animal name on the list that follows.

1. .... This animal huddles with other birds to keep warm. It uses its flippers to swim.

2. .... This flightless bird runs very fast. It kicks other animals to protect itself. It also has sharp talons.

3. .... This animal runs very fast. It runs from predators and runs to catch its dinner. Its fur blends in with nature.

4. .... This animal has a really long neck. It can reach high up in the trees.

5. .... This animal blends in with the snow. Its thick fur helps it keep warm.

6. .... This animal's long nose keeps it cool by allowing it to spray water and sand on its body.

7. .... This bird has long talons to pick up its prey. Its beak helps break up its food.

8. .... This animal can store water for days. This helps it stay hydrated in the hot weather.

Choices

A. Cheetah

B. Ostrich

C. Polar bear

D. Camel

E. Penguin

F. Eagle

G. Giraffe

H. Elephant

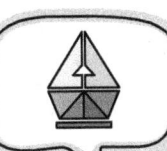
Yesterday, you experimented with matching animals to their adaptations. Today you will elaborate on the idea of adaptations and how they help animals and plants survive.

Directions: Answer the following questions.

1. Do all animals have the same traits? Why or why not?

....

....

....

....

2. Do you think the habitat where an animal lives influences its adaptations? If so, how?

....

....

....

....

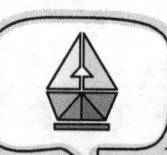
3. Would adaptations related to swimming be helpful for an animal that lives on land? Why or why not?

....

....

....

....

4. Do plants also have adaptations?

   A. Yes

   B. No

5. What adaptations do you wish you had?

....

....

....

....

WEEK 12

Life Science

The Sun and Light On Earth

2-ESS1-1

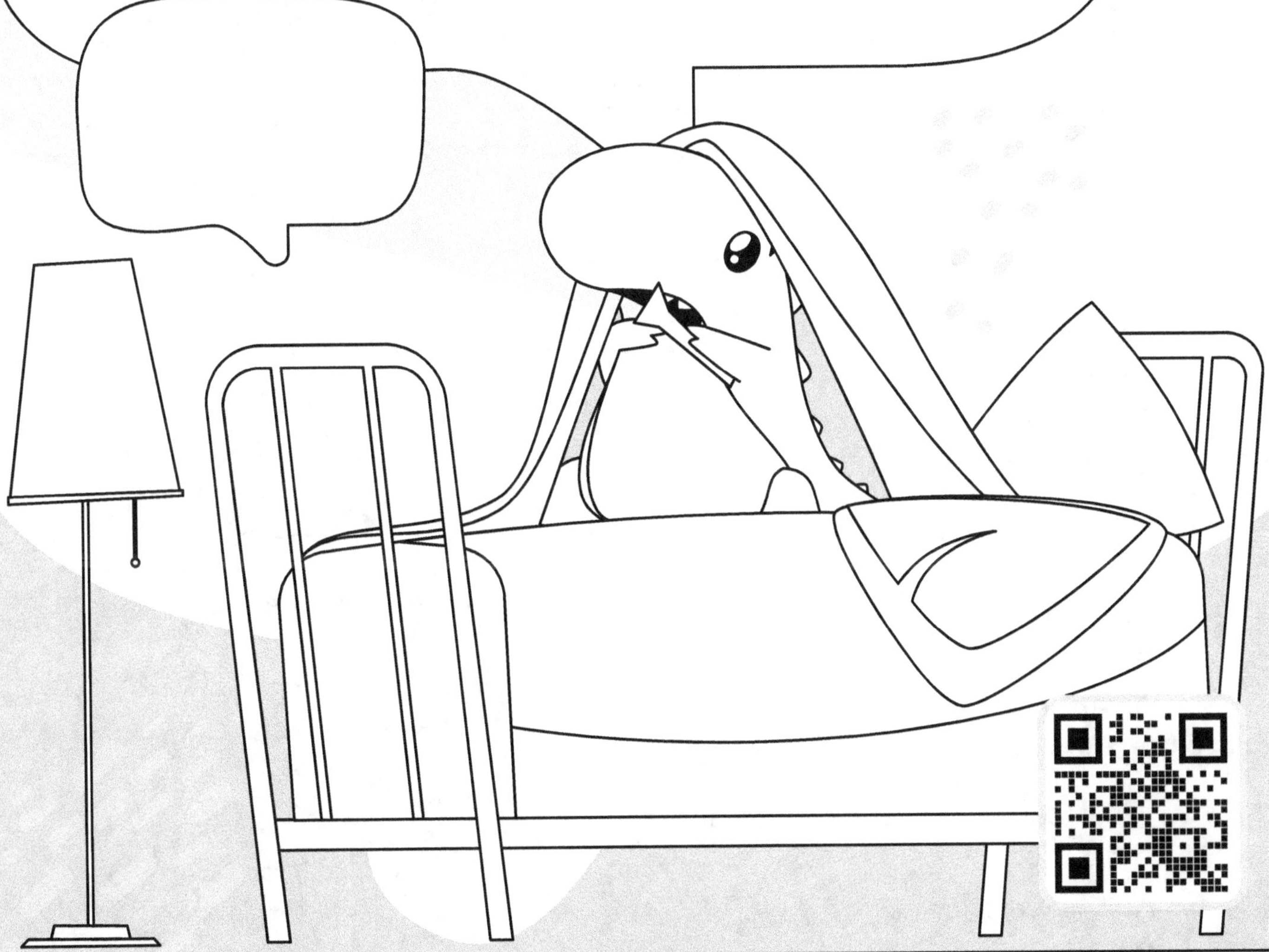

Describe the importance of the sun and what it provides the Earth.

ARGOPREP

Directions: Read the text below. Then answer the questions that follow.

The Sun: A Large Star

Did you know that our sun is actually a large star? The sun is more than one hundred times bigger than our planet! People depend on the sun. We need it in order to live because it allows plants to grow, warms the earth and controls the weather.

The sun also creates shadows. A shadow is made when an object is in the way of the sun or another light source. When the sun is low in the sky, the shadows are long. When the sun is high in the sky, the shadows are short.

When it is night time, the light from the sun disappears. Is the sun always there? Yes! The Earth rotates, or spins, even though we cannot feel it happening. When the Earth rotates, part of it faces away from the sun. When the part of the Earth on which you live faces away from the sun, it is night time for you. The sun rises in the morning, hovers directly above us in the afternoon, and sets at night. This is because of the rotation of the Earth. The sun can be seen in another part of the world while it is night where you live.

1. What type of object is the sun?

   A. A star

   B. A planet

   C. A meteor

   D. A moon

2. When an object blocks the light coming from the sun, what is made?

   A. Luminosity

   B. Night time

   C. Brightness

   D. Shadow

3. What causes the sun to rise and set every day?

   A. The weather

   B. The rotation of the Earth

   C. Shadows

   D. The moon

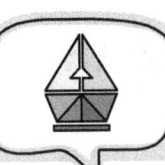
Yesterday, you learned about how the Earth's rotation causes the sun to rise and set, as well as how shadows work. Today you will explore the sun in more depth.

Directions: Ask a parent or guardian to go outside with you and observe the sun. Take two pieces of paper and a pencil with you. Be careful not to look directly at it, but rather, glance at it with sunglasses on or with glasses made specifically for viewing an eclipse. Answer the questions that follow.

1. Describe what the sun looks like.

2. Why is the size of the sun important? How does its size help the Earth in terms of light and heat?

3. With your pencil, make a small hole into the paper. Hold that paper up and let that hole and light shine through to the other piece of paper on the ground. Describe what you see.

4. Sketch the shadow that you see on the paper. What does your picture look like?

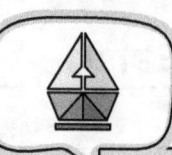
Yesterday, you explored the sun and how it is related to light and shadows. Today you will explain how shadows look, as well as how they change throughout the day.

Directions: Complete the activity about shadows. Then, answer the questions that follow.

Materials Needed:

1. a plastic cup
2. a flashlight
3. a piece of white paper

Place a piece of white paper on a table. Put the plastic cup on top of the white paper. Shut the lights off in the room and shine your flashlight on the cup.

1. What happened when you shined your light on the cup?

....

....

2. Practice moving your flashlight around to different angles and heights. What did you observe?

....

....

3. If a shadow is long, the sun is .... in the sky.

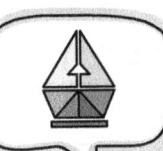
4. If a shadow is short, the sun is .... in the sky.

5. What did you learn about shadows after completing this activity?

....

....

....

....

6. Shadows are made by:

　A. The sun

　B. A source of light

　C. Both A and B

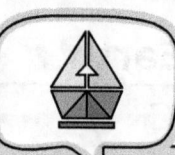
Yesterday, you explored how shadows change throughout the day. Today you will consider the sunrise and sunset and how they affect plants and animals on Earth.

Directions: Go online and research what time sunrise and sunset occur where you live. Then, research how plants and animals use the heat and light from the sun.

1. Where does the sun go after it sets where you live?

    A. It heats other parts of the Earth.

    B. It goes to sleep.

    C. It becomes the moon.

2. What are the benefits of the sun?

    A. It gives light to the Earth.

    B. It warms the Earth.

    C. Both a and b

3. How do plants use sunlight?

    A. They use the light as their source of food.

    B. They don't use sunlight.

    C. They use it to tan their leaves.

4. What are TWO different ways that animals (including humans) use the sun or benefit from the sun?

    ....

    ....

5. What time is sunrise tomorrow where you live?

    ....

6. What time is sunset tomorrow where you live?

    ....

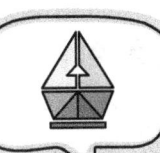
Yesterday, you researched how the sun benefits plants and animals on Earth, as well as when sunrise and sunset occur where you live. Today you will elaborate on shadows by going for an exciting shadow walk!

Directions: Complete a shadow walk and fill out the chart below. Ask someone at home to go with you. On the chart below, record each item that has a shadow. Explain if the shadow is long or short and then sketch the shadow.

Item	Is the shadow long or short?	Drawing

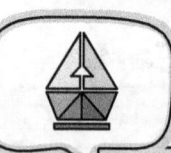
Item	Is the shadow long or short?	Drawing

1. What time of day did you go for your shadow walk?

    ....

    ....

2. Do you think shadows that are made at this time
    of day are all different lengths or the same length? Why?

    ....

    ....

    ....

    ....

WEEK 13

Earth and Space Science

Erosion

2-ESS1-1
2-ESS2-1

Explain the process of erosion and its impact on the environment.

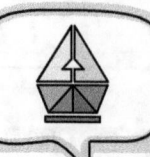
Directions: Read the passage. Then answer the questions that follow.

Water Erosion

Rain is one cause of water **erosion**, or the wearing down of landforms on Earth. Erosion can result in many negative effects on the environment. For example, heavy rainfall can harm plants and crops, cause flooding and threaten animals. When soil is washed away by heavy rains, plants may not survive. Since plants are a food source for many animals, those animals may not survive.

1. Rain is the only cause of water erosion.

   A. True
   B. False

2. Erosion is:

   A. Heavy rainfall
   B. Flooding
   C. The wearing down of landforms
   D. A food source

3. Water erosion can negatively impact:

   A. Plants
   B. Animals
   C. Crops
   D. All of the above

4. Without plants, many animals cannot survive.

   A. True
   B. False

5. Water erosion can impact an animal's:

   A. Food source
   B. Habitat
   C. Both A and B

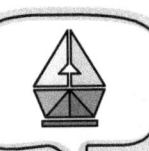
Yesterday, you learned about water erosion. Today you will explore another type of erosion - wind erosion.

Directions: Read the passage. Then answer the questions that follow.

> What is wind? Can you see it? Just because you cannot see something doesn't mean it isn't there. You can't see wind exactly, but you can see the effects of wind. You can feel the wind blowing on your skin when you are outside; you can see a kite blowing in the wind; you can see the trees and leaves moving on a windy day.
>
> Wind does a lot of things. But did you know that wind makes the waves in the ocean? It also causes tornadoes to form. Wind also breaks down rocks and mountains in a process called wind erosion.
>
> What causes wind? The Earth and the sun make the wind. The earth is tilted on its axis, and when it rotates, wind occurs.

1. Wind is a movement of ....

   A. Air

   B. Sun

   C. Oxygen

2. Wind is ....

   A. Invisible

   B. Visible

   C. Non-existent

3. What causes the wind to blow?

   ....

   ....

   ....

4. What are some events that the wind causes?

   ....

   ....

   ....

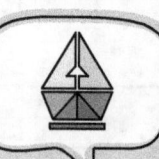
Yesterday, you explored wind erosion. Today you will complete an activity to help explain the process of wind erosion.

Directions: Complete the activity below. Then, answer the questions that follow.

Materials Needed:

1. a shoe box
2. sand (this can be craft sand)
3. a straw.

Procedure:

1. Put the sand in the box.
2. Use the straw to gently blow the sand around.
3. Repeat step #2, but this time, blow harder from one side to the other

Follow Up Questions:

1. What happened to the sand when you blew through the straw gently?

....

....

....

2. What happened to the sand when you blew through the straw harder?

....

....

....

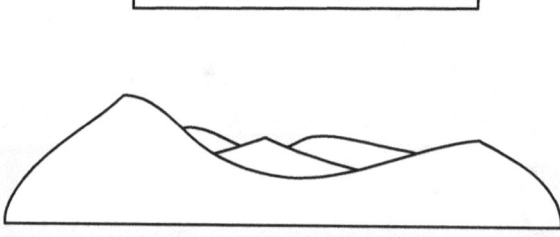

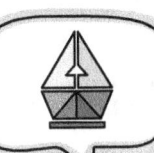

3. Think about wind erosion. What effect does wind have on sand?

....

....

....

4. How can wind erosion be a problem in nature?

....

....

....

5. What did this activity teach you about wind erosion?

....

....

....

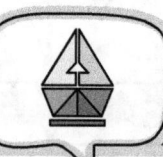
Yesterday, you explained the process of wind erosion. Today you will experiment with water erosion.

Directions: Go outdoors and complete the experiment about water erosion. Then, answer the questions that follow.

What is Water Erosion?

Erosion is the destruction or deterioration of something. Water erosion means that water slowly destroys something, usually landforms found on Earth.

Materials Needed:

1. The top of an egg carton
2. Dirt
3. Rocks or stones
4. Cup
5. Water

Procedure:

1. Fill the top of an egg carton with dirt. Be sure to pack it full.
2. Put rocks or stones on the top of the dirt.
3. Answer question #1 below.
4. Tilt the carton and soil and pour a full cup of water on the tray.
5. Answer questions #2 and 3 below.

Follow Up Questions

1. Make a prediction. You are going to angle the dirt and then pour water on it. What do you think will happen?

....

....

....

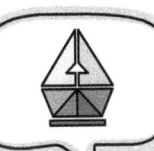
2. What does the water do to the rocks on the top of the soil?

....

....

....

3. What does the water do to the soil?

....

....

....

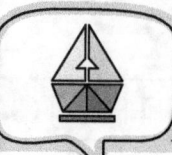
Yesterday, you experimented with water erosion. Today you will elaborate on this concept by connecting the experiment to a real-life situation.

Directions: Answer the question below. Use books or the internet to help you, if necessary.

1. What happens when water erosion occurs in nature? Is this a problem? Explain.

....

....

....

....

....

....

....

....

....

....

....

Earth and Space Science

Natural Disasters

2-ESS1-1

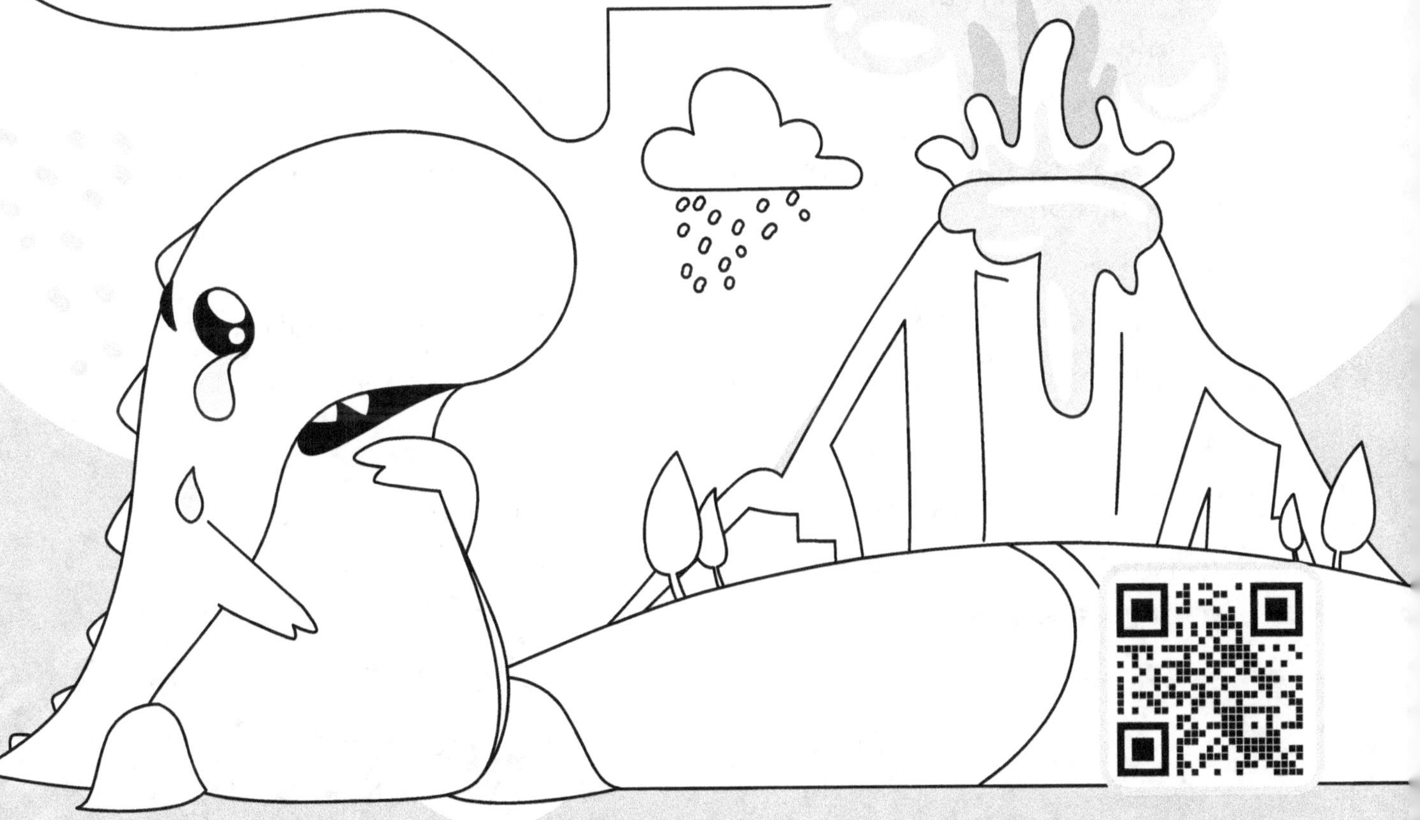

Identify a variety of natural disasters and explain their impact on the environment.

ARGOPREP

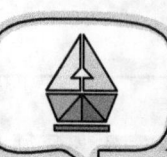
Directions: Read the passage. Then answer the questions that follow.

What is a Natural Disaster?

A **natural disaster** is an event that is caused by natural, geological processes of the Earth. These disasters cannot be avoided. Examples of common natural disasters include: tornadoes, hurricanes, floods, volcanoes and earthquakes. Natural disasters can result in the death of people and animals, as well as destruction of property such as homes, buildings and farmland. It often costs a lot of money to rebuild towns after a natural disaster strikes.

1. A natural disaster is an event that can be avoided.

    A. True   **B.** False

2. Natural disasters are caused by:

    A. Storms   **C.** Geological processes
    B. Floods   **D.** The Earth

3. Which of the following can be the result of a natural disaster? Circle <u>all</u> correct answers.

    A. Death   **C.** Volcanoes
    B. Ruined farmland   **D.** Damage to buildings

4. It costs a lot of money to rebuild a town after a natural disaster.

    A. True   **B.** False

5. Which of the following is NOT an example of a natural disaster?

    A. Hurricane
    B. Thunderstorm
    C. Tornado

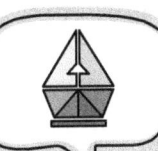
Yesterday, you learned about natural disasters. Today you will explore a specific type of natural disaster - earthquakes.

Directions: Read the passage. Then answer the questions that follow.

> **Earthquakes** happen all over the world and can be very dangerous. They cause the ground to shake. This is the result of **seismic waves** moving through the Earth. These waves occur when **tectonic plates** under the Earth move past one another. Think of tectonic plates like large puzzle pieces made up of land in the Earth. These puzzle pieces, or tectonic plates, can bump into one another and cause a seismic wave which causes the ground to shake.
>
> The first movement of an earthquake felt on Earth is called the main shock. The movements felt after the main shock are called aftershocks. Some earthquakes are so light that no one even knows they happen, but some earthquakes can be extremely dangerous. They can damage property and hurt people.
>
> Earthquakes that occur near the ocean can result in a tsunami. A **tsunami** is a very large ocean wave that can cause massive flooding and destruction when it reaches the shore.

1. What causes the ground to shake?

    A. Tectonic plates

    B. Tsunamis

    C. Seismic waves

2. What causes seismic waves?

    A. Tsunamis

    B. Tectonic plates

    C. Aftershocks

3. What are the possible effects of earthquakes?

    A. Destruction of property

    B. Injury or death of human

    C. Both A and B

4. Tsunamis occur near ....

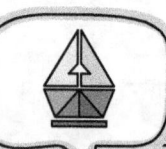
Yesterday, you explored earthquakes in more depth. Today you will learn more about another natural disaster - volcanoes.

Directions: Fill out the first section of the KWL chart below. Then, read the passage below and complete the remaining sections of the KWL chart.

> A **volcano** may look like a mountain, but it is very different from a mountain. A volcano has an opening at the top, and inside is a very hot liquid called **magma**. At times, magma can come out of the opening at the top of a volcano. This is when the volcano erupts or explodes.
>
> When the magma reaches the top of the volcano and flows out, it is called **lava**. Volcanic eruptions are very dangerous. The lava comes out of the volcano and flows down into towns. This can be harmful to people and animals because the lava can destroy property. The lava is also very hot and gives off an odor that makes it hard to breathe. It is hard to know when a volcano is going to erupt which makes them even more dangerous.

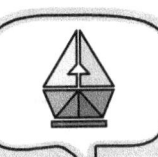
What I Already Know About Volcanoes	What I Still Want To Know About Volcanoes	What I Learned About Volcanoes After Reading

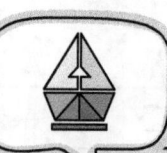
Yesterday, you learned about volcanoes. Today you will conduct an experiment to create your own volcano.

Directions: Complete the experiment below. Then, answer the questions that follow.

Materials Needed:

1. 5 tablespoons vinegar
2. $\frac{1}{3}$ cup water
3. 4 teaspoons baking soda
4. 2 teaspoons dish soap
5. 3 drops red food coloring
6. 2 bowls
7. a pan
8. paper towels

Procedure:

1. In one bowl, stir the baking soda, dish soap and water.
2. In another bowl, add the vinegar and food coloring.
3. Place the bowl of baking soda, dish soap and water inside a rectangular pan. This is just to catch any drips.
4. Pour the vinegar and food coloring slowly into the other bowl.

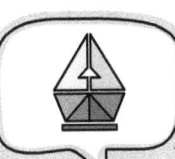
Follow Up Questions

1. What happened when you mixed the ingredients from the two bowls together?

....

....

....

2. Did the reaction occur quickly or slowly?

....

....

....

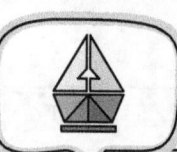
Yesterday, you experimented with creating a volcano. Today you will elaborate on this concept by connecting the experiment to a real volcano.

Directions: Answer the question below. Use books or the internet to help you, if necessary.

1. Explain how the experiment you conducted yesterday is similar to a real volcano erupting.

....

....

....

....

....

....

....

....

....

....

....

WEEK 15

Earth and Space Science

Seasons

2-ESS1-1

Identify the similarities and differences between the four seasons.

ARGOPREP

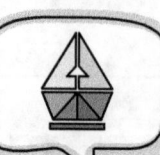
Directions: Read the passage. Then answer the questions that follow.

Why are There Four Seasons?

Why do we have different seasons? Why isn't it just always summer or always winter? We have seasons because the Earth **orbits**, or travels around the sun. It takes the Earth one year to travel around the sun one time.

As the Earth travels around the sun, we transition through different seasons. These seasons are tied to certain weather patterns. When a certain part of the Earth is closer to the sun, it is summer. During the summer, it is the hottest, and the sun shines more. When that same part of Earth is tilted away from the sun, it becomes winter. Winter is when we get the least amount of sun. When it is summer on one side of our planet, it is winter on the other side.

Just as the seasons change, so does our weather. It is colder and the days are shorter in winter. In the summer, the days are longer and the sun shines more, bringing warmer temperatures.

1. When the Earth is tilted toward the sun, the season is ....

2. When the Earth is tilted away from the sun, the season is ....

3. How long does it take the Earth to orbit the sun?

   A. 1 season

   B. 1 month

   C. 1 year

4. How can it be summer in the United States but winter in Brazil? Explain

   ....

   ....

5. What does the word orbit mean?

   ....

   ....

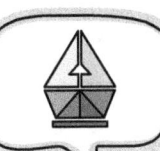
Yesterday, you learned why there are four seasons. Today you will explore the most common types of weather during each season.

Directions: Read the passage. Then answer the questions that follow.

"

Depending on where you live, the weather during each season may be slightly different. In most parts of the United States, winter is the coldest and wettest season, and summer is the hottest and driest season. Spring and autumn usually fall somewhere in between.

In many parts of the United States, temperatures drop and snow falls during winter. People dress warmly, bundling up in coats, hats and mittens to go outdoors. However, in some other parts of the country, the weather is much milder during winter.

The same holds true for summer. In some areas of the country, the temperatures can be extremely hot with little rainfall while other areas experience milder temperatures during the summer.

"

1. Which season usually brings cooler temperatures?

    A. Summer

    B. Winter

2. Which season is typically the driest?

    A. Winter

    B. Spring

    C. Summer

    D. Fall

3. The difference in weather during different seasons depends on:

    A. The season

    B. Your location

    C. The temperature

    D. Rainfall

4. All areas in the United States experience the same weather during each season.

    A. True

    B. False

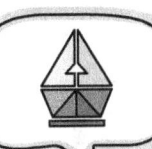
Yesterday, you explored common types of weather during each season. Today you will explain the characteristics of each season where you live.

Directions: On the table below, describe the weather that occurs during each season where you live.

FALL	WINTER

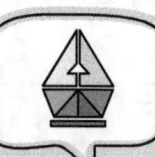
SPRING	SUMMER

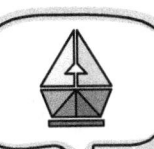

Yesterday, you described the weather during each season where you live. Today you will learn more about a specific weather event - blizzards.

Directions: Read the passage below. Then, answer the questions that follow.

> A winter snowstorm results from the difference in temperature and the moisture in the air. When these differences meet, it causes a **cold front**. During a cold front, snow falls. Snow occurs when water vapor changes to ice. This happens when the temperature falls below 32 degrees.
>
> Some winter snowstorms turn into blizzards. A **blizzard** is a winter snowstorm that lasts for several days or more. Blizzards have strong winds and heavy snow that accumulates, or adds up, very quickly. Blizzards can be very dangerous because they make it difficult to drive or get around.

1. How is a winter snowstorm different from a blizzard?

....

....

2. What is a cold front?

....

....

....

3. What happens during a blizzard?

....

....

....

Yesterday, you learned more about blizzards. Today you will elaborate on this concept by connecting the reading to a real-life experience.

Directions: Answer the question below. Use books or the internet to help you, if necessary.

1. Have you ever experienced a blizzard where you live? If so, describe what it was like. If not, describe what you think might happen in your hometown.

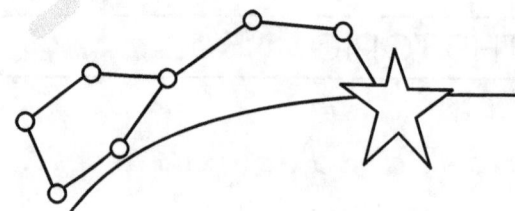

WEEK 16

Earth and Space Science

Parts of the Solar System

2-ESS1-1

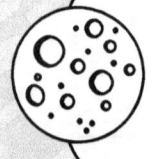

Identify different parts of the solar system and how they interact with one another.

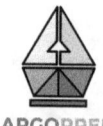

ARGOPREP

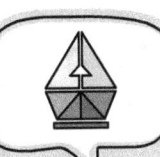
Directions: Read the passage. Then answer the questions that follow.

The Solar System

The solar system is made up of many parts. The largest object in the solar system is the Sun. Many smaller objects are connected to the sun by **gravity**, and they orbit, or travlel, around the sun. These objects include planets, moons, asteroids, meteoroids and comets, all of which are part of the solar system. Our solar system is part of the galaxy, the Milky Way. It is the only solar system known to support life. Scientists and astronauts have spent many decades trying to learn as much as possible about our solar system.

1. List the 6 parts of the solar system.

A. ....

B. ....

C. ....

D. ....

E. ....

F. ....

2. All smaller parts of the solar system orbit the:

A. Sun

B. Galaxy

C. Moon

D. Milky Way

3. Our solar system is the only one known to support life.

A. True

B. False

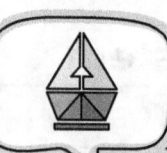
Yesterday, you learned about the parts of the solar system. Today you will explore one planet, Mercury, in more depth.

Directions: Read the passage. Then answer the questions that follow.

The planet Mercury is the closest planet to the sun. If you were able to stand on this planet, the sun would look bigger than it does from Earth. This is because Mercury is closer to the sun than Earth. This means the sun appears brighter and feels hotter on Mercury than it does on Earth.

Life on Mercury is very different from life on Earth. It is very dry and has craters similar to the moon. The two planets do have one thing in common, though! Both have a north and south pole that is made primarily of ice. This is because these portions of the Mercury and Earth are not near the sun.

1. Which planet is closer to the sun?

    A. Earth

    B. Mercury

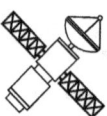
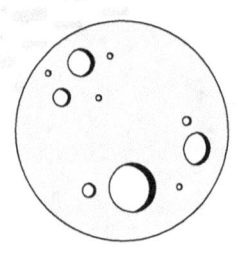

2. If you were standing on Mercury, would the sun appear:

    A. Smaller

    B. Larger

3. Describe at least one difference between Mercury and the planet Earth?

    ....

    ....

    ....

4. Describe at least one similarity between Mercury and the planet Earth?

    ....

    ....

    ....

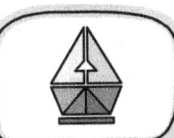
Yesterday, you explored the planet, Mercury. Today you will learn about and explain the concept of a solar eclipse.

Directions: Read the passage below. Then, answer the questions that follow.

A Solar Eclipse

A solar eclipse happens when the moon moves directly in front of the sun, creating a shadow on the Earth. It becomes very dark during a solar eclipse; however, a small sliver of the sun can still be seen. That sliver of light is very bright and can be harmful to your eyes.

Solar eclipses have been recorded by scientists for many years. They date back to ancient times. Back then, many people thought that a solar eclipse was a sign that something bad would happen, but now scientists know that they occur because the moon and the sun temporarily align. Solar eclipses only occur every few years.

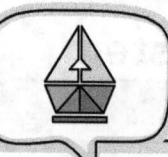
1. In your own words, what is a solar eclipse?

....

....

....

2. In ancient times, what did people believe about a solar eclipse?

    A. The sun and moon temporarily align

    B. They imply something bad will happen

    C. A storm is coming

3. Why does a solar eclipse actually happen?

    A. The sun and moon temporarily align

    B. Something bad will happen

    C. A storm is coming

4. What is something you should never do during a solar eclipse?

....

....

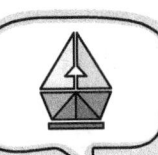
Yesterday, you learned about and explained the concept of a solar eclipse. Today you will experiment with this concept by making a solar eclipse viewer.

Directions: Complete the activity below. Then, answer the questions that follow.

1. Using what you learned in the previous lesson, explain why you should not look at the sun during a solar eclipse.

....

....

Materials Needed:

1. A shoebox
2. Tape
3. Scissors
4. Aluminum foil
5. A piece of white paper

Procedure:

1. Cut the white paper to fit one side of the shoebox. Use the tape to secure it.
2. On the other side of the shoe box, cut two holes on opposite ends of the box.
3. Cover the hole on the left side with aluminum foil. Use tape to secure it.
4. Use the scissors to poke a hole in the aluminum foil.

This solar eclipse viewer can be used to look at the sun on a normal day, not just during a solar eclipse.

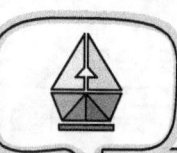
Directions:

Put your back to the sun. Hold the viewer up and look through one of the holes.

2. What do you see when you look through the box?

....

....

....

3. What is the purpose of the hole in the aluminum foil?

....

....

....

4. How does this viewer help you look at the sun?

....

....

....

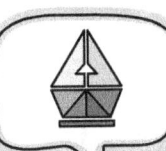
Yesterday, you made a solar eclipse viewer. Today you will elaborate on this concept by learning more about one part of the solar system.

Directions: Choose one object that is found in our solar system. Use books or the internet to learn more about it. Describe what you learned below.

WEEK 17

Earth and Space Science

Water on Earth

2-ESS2-2
2-ESS2-3

Identify where water is found on Earth and that it can be in solid or liquid form.

ARGOPREP

Directions: Read the passage. Then answer the questions that follow.

Water is essential to all forms of life on planet Earth. Without water, plants and animals would not be able to survive. Fortunately, nearly 75% of the Earth's surface is covered by water. This water comes in the form of saltwater, like the water found in the world's five oceans, and freshwater, the water found in lakes, rivers and streams.

Water is used on our planet in a variety of ways. It is used for drinking, growing crops, and extinguishing fires. It is even used as a source of power in some areas. Ensuring the water supply on our planet is very important!

1. List the 5 oceans on Earth. Use books or the internet, if necessary.

A. ....

B. ....

C. ....

D. ....

E. ....

2. Water is essential to:

A. Plants

B. Animals

C. All forms of life

3. What percentage of the Earth's surface is NOT covered by water?

A. 75%

B. 50%

C. 25%

D. 0%

4. Water can be used as a source of power.

A. True

B. False

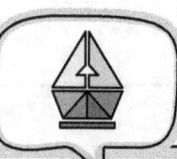
Yesterday, you learned about the importance of water on our planet. Today you will explore watersheds.

Directions: Read the passage. Then answer the questions that follow.

> The portion of land that drains into a body of water is called a **watershed**. Water goes directly into a water system, such as rivers, lakes and oceans, when it rains or when water drips down from mountains or hills. Water that is collected in smaller bodies of water eventually ends up in the ocean. This is because small bodies of water, such as creeks, feed into medium-sized bodies of water, such as lakes and rivers, which feed into larger bodies of water, like the ocean.
>
> The Continental Divide splits North America in half. The water that is west of the Continental Divide ends up in the Pacific Ocean. The water that is east of the Continental Divide ends up in the Atlantic Ocean.
>
> While the water travels, it can collect elements that end up in the water supply. For example, if the water reaches the roads, it might collect the salt that is used to melt snow and ice in wintertime. Water can also collect pesticides if it travels through farmland.

1. In your own words, explain what a watershed is.

....

....

2. Where does rainwater end up?

....

....

3. The Continental Divide splits North America in half from:

   A. North to south

   B. East to west

   C. Large to small

4. What are examples of unnatural elements that can be collected in water as it travels?

....

....

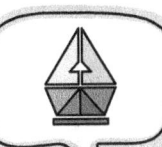
Yesterday, you explored the concept of watersheds. Today you will learn more about the watersheds where you live.

Directions: Answer the questions below.

1. Where do you live?

_____

_____

_____

2. Name some rivers or lakes located near where you live.

A. _____

B. _____

C. _____

3. Based on where you live and what you know about the Continental Divide, into which ocean does water in your area flow?

_____

_____

_____

_____

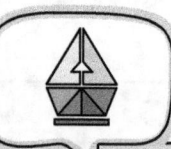
4. What unnatural elements do you think the water will collect on its way from where you live to the ocean? (ex. Salt, pesticides, etc.)

....

....

....

Ask an adult to help you visit the EPA's website listed below. Enter your zip code. The website will list watersheds in your area and provide information on whether or not they are polluted. Write this information below.

https://watersgeo.epa.gov/mywaterway/search.html

5. Watershed: ....

Is it polluted? ....

Watershed: ....

Is it polluted? ....

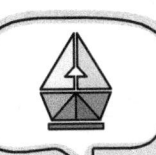
Yesterday, you learned about the watersheds in your area. Today you will conduct an experiment with water.

Directions: Complete the activity below. Then, answer the questions that follow.

1. Can ice grow bigger? Make a prediction below.

....

....

Materials Needed:

1. A plastic cup
2. Water
3. Freezer

Procedure:

• Fill the plastic cup with water all the way to the top.

• Place the cup of water in the freezer for 12-24 hours.

2. What do you think will happen to the water in the cup?

....

....

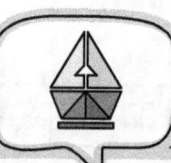
- Remove the cup of water from the freezer and observe.

3. Describe what you observe.

....

....

- Place the cup in the sink.

- Fill another cup with cool water.

- Slowly pour the cool water over the cup of ice.

4. What happens?

....

....

5. Describe what you see in the cup.

....

....

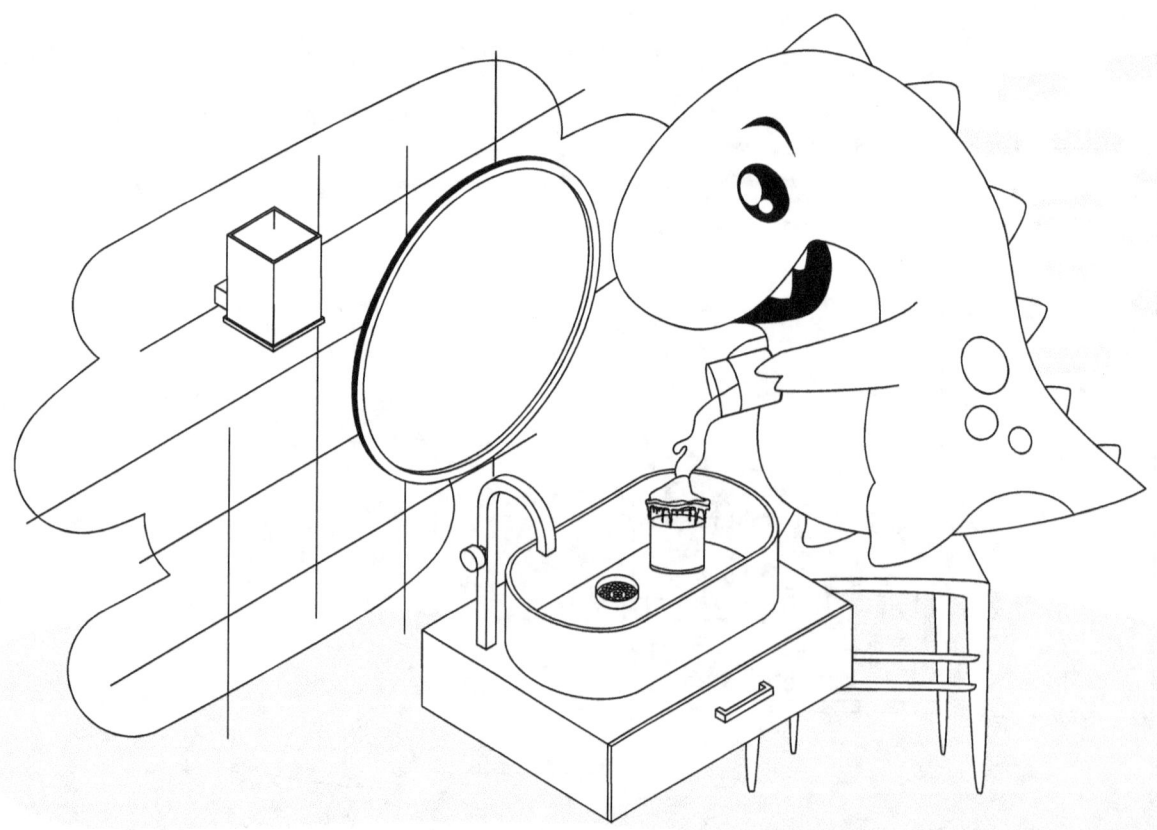

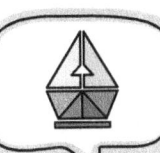
Yesterday, you conducted an experiment to determine whether or not water can grow. Today you will elaborate on this concept by learning more about glaciers.

Directions: Read the passage about glaciers. Then, answer the questions that follow.

"

Glaciers are thick sheets and mountains of ice that are found in the ocean. They can range in size from very small to incredibly large. Some glaciers are flat and look like land that is covered with snow. Other glaciers are large and look like hills or mountains. Some glaciers can even be pointy. Regardless of how big or small a glacier is, the ice is a thick layer and can extend deep into the ocean.

Glaciers move through the cold oceans; however, they do not move very fast. Some glaciers move just a few inches a day.

"

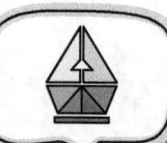
1. How fast do glaciers move in the ocean?

....

....

2. Do all glaciers look alike? Explain.

....

....

....

3. How might glaciers be dangerous to boats in the ocean?

....

....

....

4. If you stood on top of a glacier, do you think you would risk falling through the ice? Explain why or why not.

....

....

....

5. After reading this passage and completing the previous lesson, how do you think glaciers grow?

....

....

....

WEEK 18

Earth and Space Science

Taking Care of Our Planet

K-2-ETS1-1
2-ESS1-1

 Identify ways in which people can care for the planet.

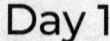
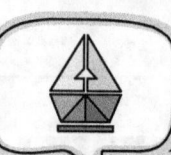
Directions: Read the passage. Then answer the questions that follow.

"
> Our Earth provides us with many things that are essential to life. The air we breathe, the plants we grow for food and the water we drink all come from nature. It is important that we care for the planet so that these things are available to people for generations to come.
>
> Unfortunately, we do many things that are harmful to the environment. This includes things like wasting water, using single-use plastics and putting pollution into the air. All of these habits can be reversed, however, with a few simple acts like recycling and conserving water, when possible.
>
> Hopefully, if we all do our small part now, future generations will be able to enjoy all the Earth has to offer!
"

1. List 3 things humans get from the Earth.

　　A. ....

　　B. ....

　　C. ....

2. List 3 things humans do that are harmful to the Earth.

　　A. ....

　　B. ....

　　C. ....

3. There are things we can do now to help protect our planet.

　　A. True

　　B. False

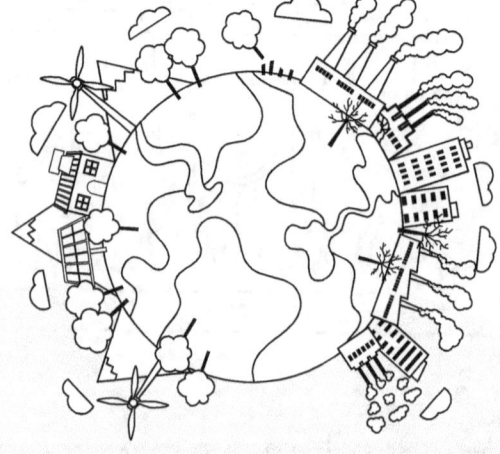

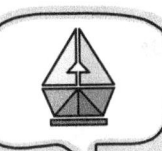
Yesterday, you learned about the importance of taking care of our planet. Today you will explore recycling.

Directions: Read the passage below. Then, identify which of the items on the list below can be recycled. Circle those items.

> Recycling has many benefits. Recycling helps eliminate some of the trash that winds up in landfills. Landfills are where the garbage goes after it is collected by the garbage truck.
>
> Unfortunately, landfills are filling up too quickly, not only with trash but also with materials that can be recycled. Recyclable materials include plastics, paper, aluminum cans and glass. Not only does recycling prevent landfills from becoming overfilled, but it also saves money and energy because recycled items can be turned into other materials that people can use.

1. Which of the following items can be recycled?

1. Soda cans

2. A hamburger

3. Diaper

4. Glass bottles

5. Milk carton

6. Foam

7. Plastic water bottle

8. Notebook paper

9. Motor oil

10. Newspaper

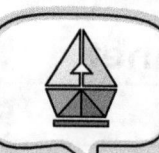
Yesterday, you explored the concept of recycling. Today you will learn more about another way to care for the environment - composting.

Directions: Read the passage below. Then, answer the questions that follow.

> **Composting** is the process of decomposing certain materials into compost, a nutrient-rich fertilizer. The word decomposed means that something can be broken down. Think about the food items that are thrown away at the end of a meal. Most of these foods, including fruits and vegetables, can be put in a compost pile rather than the garbage can. The same can be done with dead plants from the garden.
>
> How does composting work? When you put natural materials, like fruits, vegetables and plants, in a compost pile, they will slowly break down into the dirt. The compost will eventually turn into fertilizer and mulch that can be used in your garden. The compost will help save space in landfills and help the plants in your garden grow!

1. In your own words, what is composting?

....
....

2. How is composting similar to recycling?

....
....

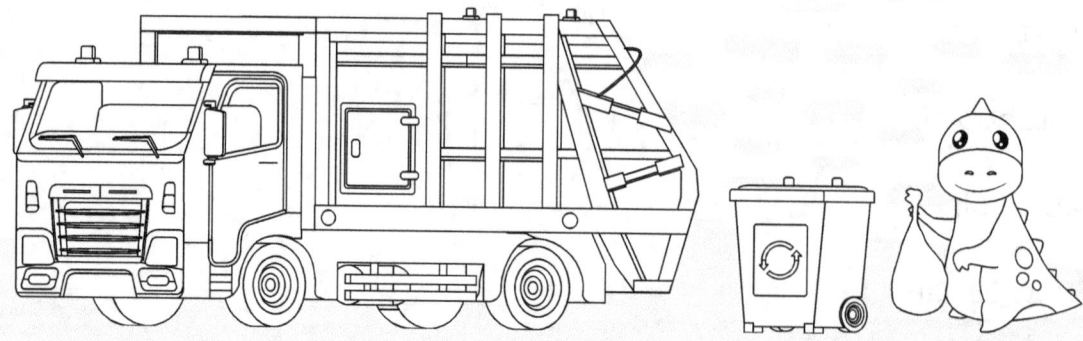

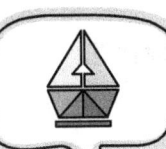
3. How is composting different from recycling?

....

....

....

4. What items can be used in a compost pile?

....

....

....

5. What items cannot be used in a compost pile?

....

....

....

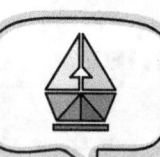
Yesterday, you learned about composting and compared and contrasted it with recycling. Today you will classify materials by whether they should be composted or recycled.

Directions: Read the list below. Decide whether the material should be composted or recycled. Place a check mark in the correct box. In the empty rows at the bottom of the table, list 4 materials and identify whether they should be composted or recycled.

Material	Composted	Recycled
Grass clippings		
Paper		
Potato skins		
Broccoli stalks		
Banana peel		
Cardboard boxes		
Withered flowers		
Apple		
Orange peel		

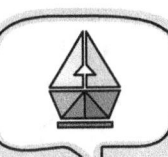
Material	Composted	Recycled
Soda can		
Plastic water bottle		

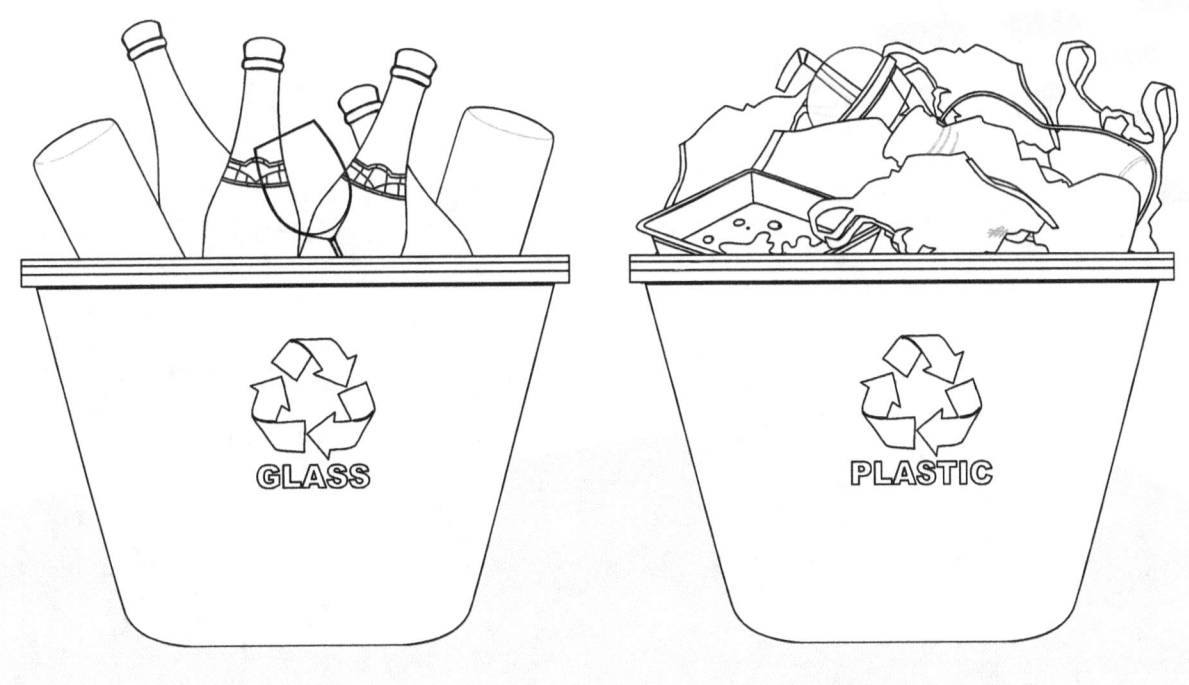

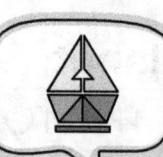
Yesterday, you decided whether materials should be composted or recycled. Today you will learn about one other way to help our environment and make connections to your own life.

Directions: Read the passage below. Then, answer the questions that follow.

"

The word conservation means to save. Why might it be important to save water? Even though it may seem like there is a lot of water on our planet, in many parts of the world, people do not have access to clean water.

Plants and animals all rely on water to live as well. Water is a resource we need to conserve, and there are many easy ways to do just that. How can you save water?

"

Directions: List 5 ways you can save water in your everyday life.

1. ....
2. ....
3. ....
4. ....
5. ....

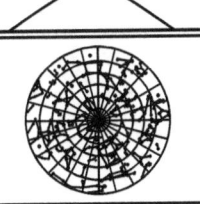

WEEK 19

Earth and Space Science

The Day and Night Sky

2-ESS1-1

Understand and explain the phases of the moon, as well as similarities and differences between the day sky and night sky.

ARGOPREP

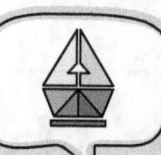
Directions: Fill out the first column on the KWL chart below. Then, read the passage and fill out the remaining columns on the KWL chart.

Have you ever noticed that the sun comes up in one direction and goes down in another direction? Throughout the day, the sun changes its position in the sky. When the sun comes up on Earth, it is called sunrise. The sun always rises from the East. When the sun goes down for the day, it is called sunset. The sun always sets in the West.

If you track the sun throughout the day, it appears as if it is moving slowly across the sky. However, the sun is not moving at all! It just looks like it is. In reality, the Earth is moving. We cannot feel the Earth moving because it moves so slowly. As the Earth turns, we see the sun from different positions, making it appear as though the sun is moving across the sky.

What Did You Already Know About The Day and Night Sky Before Reading This Passage?	What Do You Still Want To Know About This Topic?	What Did You Learn After Reading This Passage?

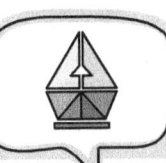
Yesterday, you learned about how the sun rises and sets. Today you will further explore the sky.

Directions: Use your prior knowledge to answer the questions below.

1. The .... is a large yellow ball made of gas.

   A. The moon
   B. The sun
   C. Saturn

2. Is the sun bigger or smaller than the Earth?

   ....

   ....

   ....

3. The sun is a ....

   A. Star
   B. Planet
   C. Moon

4. What needs the sun in order to live?

   A. Dirt
   B. Water
   C. Plants

5. The moon gives off light AND heats the Earth.

   A. True
   B. False

6. The surface of the moon is:

   A. Covered in water
   B. Grassy
   C. Hot
   D. Rocky

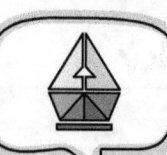
Yesterday, you explored objects in the sky. Today you will learn more about the phases of the moon.

Directions: Read the information about the different phases of the moon on the left side of the table below. Then, draw pictures to match the descriptions on the right side.

MOON PHASE	DRAWING
Waxing Crescent A small portion of the moon's right side shows light.	
Full Moon The entire moon shows light.	
Last Quarter The left half of the moon is lit.	

MOON PHASE	DRAWING
Waxing Gibbous About $\frac{3}{4}$ of the moon is lit.	
Waning Crescent A tiny part of the moon's left side shows light.	
1st Quarter The right half of the moon is lit.	

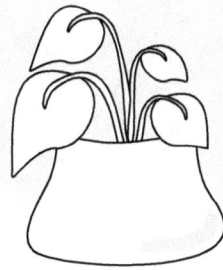

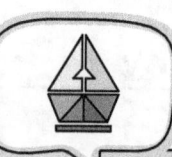
Yesterday, you learned about the phases of the moon. Today you will make observations about the sun.

Directions: Complete the activity below. Then, answer the questions that follow.

Materials Needed:

1. A window
2. A white piece of paper
3. Tape
4. Writing utensil

Procedure:

• Find a window in your house that lets a lot of light in. In the morning, go to that window and locate the sun.

1. What does the sun look like? Where is it located in the sky?

....

....

....

- Tape the piece of paper to the window and trace the sun.

2. Where is the piece of paper located on the window (high, low)?

....

....

....

- Use the Internet to find out what time the sun sets today. Then, about fifteen minutes before that time, return to the window.

3. Is the sun in the same place as the tracing on the paper?

    A. Yes

    B. No

4. Where is the sun located in the sky now?

....

....

....

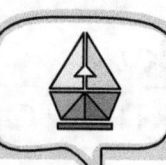
Yesterday, you made observations about the sun. Today you will elaborate on what you have learned this week.

Directions: Answer the questions below.

1. List 3 things you learned about the day sky.

   A. ....

   B. ....

   C. ....

2. List 3 things you learned about the night sky.

   A. ....

   B. ....

   C. ....

3. What do the sun and the moon have in common?

....

....

....

....

Engineering

Solve a Problem

K-2-ETS1-1
K-2-ETS1-2

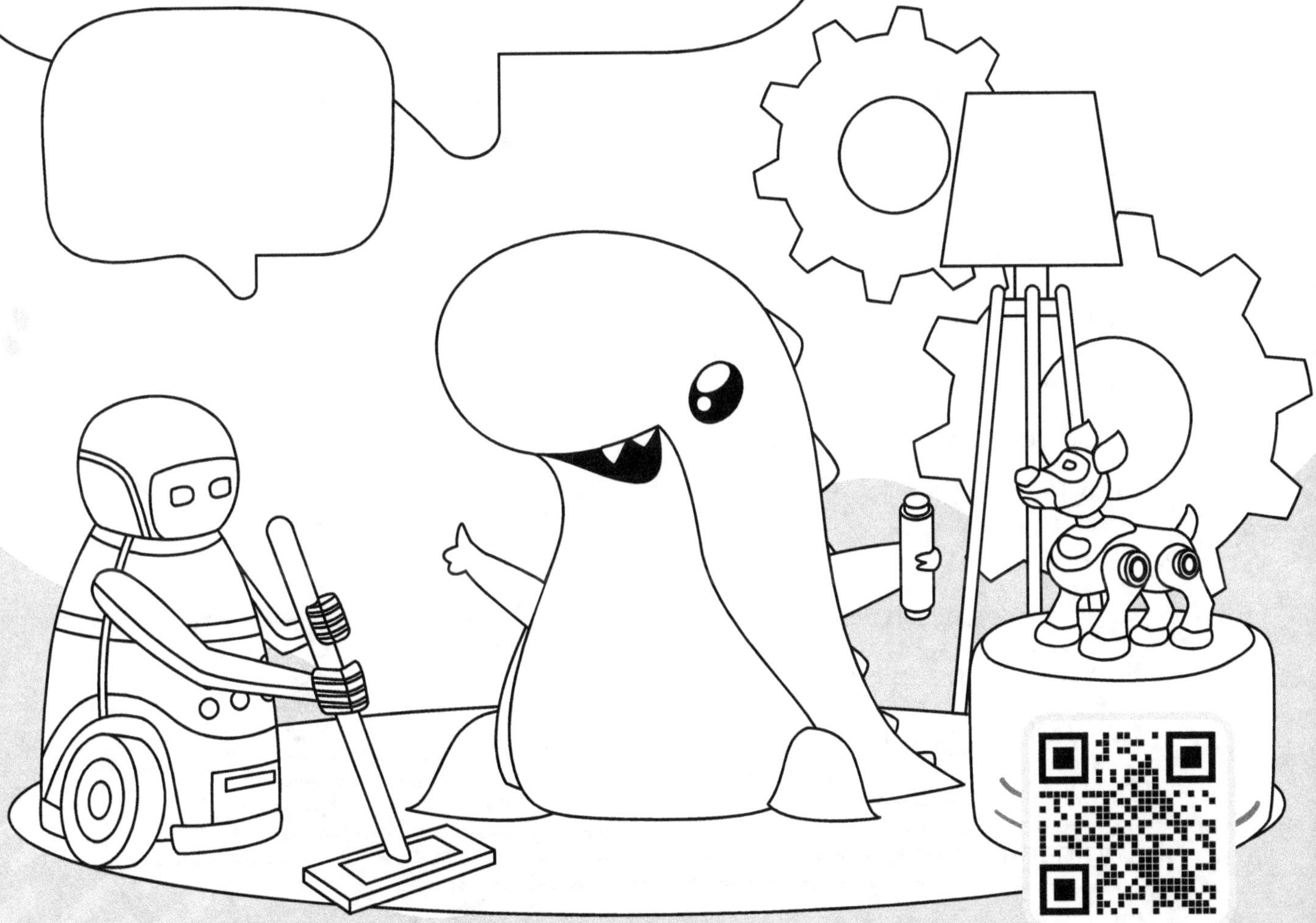

Gather information to identify a simple problem that can be solved through the development of a robot.

Directions: Read the passage below. Then, answer the questions that follow.

What is Engineering?

Engineering is the process of designing, creating and building things using math and science. An engineer, or person who does the engineering, makes observations, asks questions and collects data in order to figure out the best way to build something. Engineers also fulfill needs or wants and solve problems by designing a product or system as a solution to the problem. They often have to complete these projects with certain materials, within a given time period and/or with a set budget.

1. Engineers are probably good scientists and mathematicians.

    A. True

    B. False

2. Engineers:

    A. Fulfill needs

    B. Fulfill wants

    C. Solve problems

    D. All of the above

3. Engineers often have to:

    A. Work with certain materials

    B. Work on deadlines

    C. Work on a budget

    D. All of the above

4. Engineers are problem solvers.

    A. True

    B. False

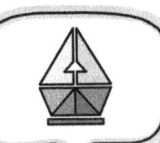
Yesterday, you learned about engineering. Today you will further explore one type of machine that engineers create - robots.

Directions: Read the passage below. Then, answer the questions that follow. <u>**Use the Internet to help you answer questions 1 - 5.**</u>

> What are robots? **Robots** are machines that complete different tasks. Engineers and scientists create robots to help humans do both simple and complex tasks. Some robots are designed to keep humans safe. Robots are also helpful because they can complete tasks much faster than humans can. Think about all the different kinds of robots in the world.

1. What is an example of a robot that helps humans around the house? How does it work?

....

....

....

2. What is an example of a robot that helps humans in factories? How does it work?

....

....

....

3. What is an example of a robot that helps humans in space? How does it work?

....

....

....

4. What is an example of a robot that helps humans in the military? How does it work?

....

....

....

5. What is an example of a robot that helps humans in the hospital? How does it work?

....

....

....

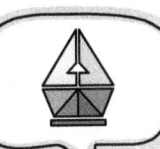
Yesterday, you explored how robots are helpful to humans. Today, you will identify a problem that could be solved by a robot that you will design.

Directions: Think about the goal of your robot design. Answer the questions below.

1. Identify the problem your robot will solve:

....

....

....

2. Identify how your robot will solve the problem:

....

....

....

3. What is the goal of your project? What should your design be able to do?

....

....

....

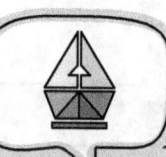
Yesterday, you identified a problem that could be solved by a robot. Today you will begin to design your robot.

Directions: Based on the problem and solution you identified yesterday, draw your own robot below. Don't forget to think like a mechanical engineer!

Name of your robot:

Yesterday, you designed your own robot. Today you will elaborate on how it solves your identified problem.

Directions: Answer the questions below.

1. How does your robot work?

....

....

....

....

....

....

2. What materials did you use to design your robot?

....

....

....

....

....

....

....

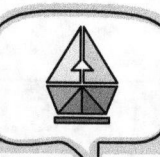

3. How will your robot solve the problem you identified?

....

....

....

....

....

....

....

Answer Sheets

To see the answer key to the entire workbook, you can easily download the answer key from our website!

*Due to the high request from parents and teachers, we have removed the answer key from the workbook so you do not need to rip out the answer key while students work on the workbook.

To watch free video explanations go to: **argoprep.com/science2**
OR scan the QR Code:

Place your mouse over the workbook you have, and you will see the "Download Answers" button.

For detailed video instructions on how to access the "Answer Sheets," please scan this QR code.

6th Grade Science: Daily Practice Workbook | 20 Weeks of Fun

3rd Grade Science: Daily Practice Workbook | 20 Weeks of Fun...

4th Grade Science: Daily Practice Workbook | 20 Weeks of Fun...

7th Grade Science: Daily Practice Workbook | 20 Weeks of Fun...

5th Grade Science: Daily Practice Workbook | 20 Weeks of Fun...

8th Grade Science: Daily Practice Workbook | 20 Weeks of Fun...

Kindergarten Science: Daily Practice Workbook | 20 Weeks of Fun...

1st Grade Science: Daily Practice Workbook | 20 Weeks of Fun...

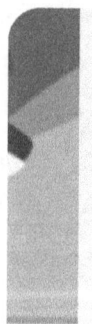

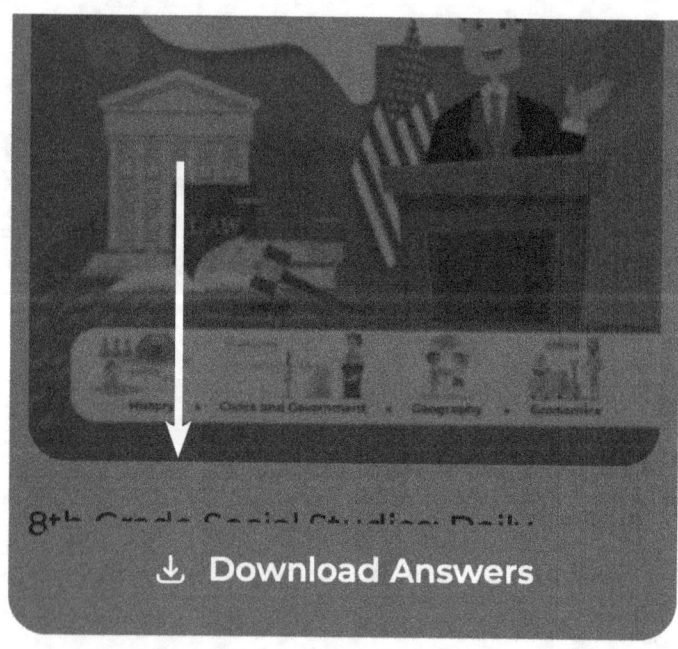

8th Grade Social Studies: Daily

⬇ Download Answers

4th Grade Social Studies: Practice Workbook